step-by-step
Golf

techniques

hamlyn

step-by-step

Golf

techniques

Derek Lawrenson

First published in Great Britain in 2002 by
Hamlyn, a division of Octopus Publishing Group Ltd
2–4 Heron Quays, London E14 4JP

Distributed in the United States and Canada by
Sterling Publishing Co., Inc.
387 Park Avenue South, New York, NY 10016-8810

ISBN 0 600 60379 2

A CIP catalogue record for this book is available from
the British Library

Printed and bound in China

10 9 8 7 6 5 4 3 2 1

Imperial Measurements
Golf remains a sport in which imperial measurements
still dominate. For reference:
1 inch = 2.54cm
1 foot = 30cm
1 yard = 0.91m

contents

INTRODUCTION

The game of golf remains one of the few major sports that is not prejudiced against the fat person or thin, the tall or small, young or old. That is why it appeals to people from across all walks of life. It can be thrilling, exhilarating, frustrating, maddening, indeed just about any adjective you care to mention. But what makes it so special is that it can be any – or all – of these things to anyone.

Hyatt Hotels once did a survey which showed that more business deals were conducted on the golf course than in the company boardroom. Other golf courses, however, are full of people who have never done a business deal in their lives but who just enjoy the game's simple pleasures.

Golf is also one of the few major sports that doesn't harbour, or encourage, cheating of any kind. There is no referee, no umpire. You are the sole judge of your actions. It is the easiest game in the world at which to cheat and that is why few people ever do it, and why being caught cheating is the worst thing that can happen to a golfer. A solicitor who was caught regularly moving his ball in the rough was not only thrown out of his local club, but his business went to pot as well. The inference was clear: his clients clearly thought that if he could cheat at golf then he must be cheating in his professional life as well.

But golf is guilty of pushing people away in other ways . It can be said that the game has an intimidating air about it. Go down to your local private club and invariably there will be a sign at the front gate stressing the 'private' bit. The sport's rules appear forbidding and convoluted. Even the players who earn millions can't understand them. Nick Faldo twice fell foul of the rules in 1994. And how long do you need to be playing to score respectably? How long before that complicated grip starts to feel comfortable? Will I ever stop slicing the ball? What

does cavity blade mean? Golf is the game that launches a thousand questions.

It is also fair to say that the sport has an expensive air to it. Golf clubs can be pricey instruments. Furthermore, if you ever pluck up the courage to get past the front entrance you may find that your local private club will be extremely expensive to join. If, that is, you can get in at all.

But golf doesn't have to be any of these things. This book sets out to demystify some of the game's language and its codes. The instruction section is easy to read and easy to follow; something not usually associated with golf instruction books. Many leave the reader confused, baffled and ready to take up something less taxing like running a marathon. Others prefer the pompous language route, whereby the 'expert' tries to impress the student with his knowledge and command of golfing terms. Do yourself a favour and forget those routes.

If you persevere, you will find the game of your dreams. You will discover that equipment need not cost a fortune, and you will find a club that is a bastion of warmth and hospitality. This book will show you what to do when your ball is buried in a bunker or lies at the bottom of a lake, and instead of fearing for your life when you hear you're playing in a tournament with a shotgun start, you'll have the time of your life.

The American sportswriter Grantland Rice got it right in 1920 when he wrote:

'Golf is about 20 per cent mechanics and technique. The other 80 per cent is philosophy, humour, tragedy, romance, melodrama, companionship, camaraderie, cussedness and conversation.'

This book will give you the first 20 per cent; it will also help on those all too frequent days when the golfing shot you can't play is sapping your morale faster than a raging toothache.

◀◀ Practice makes perfect
where golf is concerned.
Follow the tips and advice in
this book and you are sure to
improve your game.

Why Golf?

Suggest to a Scot that the game of golf was not actually invented in Scotland and you can hear the cry go up, 'What do you mean they didn't invent the game of golf? Isn't St Andrews in Fife the "Home of Golf"? Isn't the game's ruling body the Royal & Ancient Golf Club of St Andrews?'

History

Evidence that the Scots invented the game is, however, at the very least inconclusive. The 'auld grey toun' has done very well out of claiming to be the 'Home of Golf' but it may be nothing of the sort – there are several claims to the title.

Exhibit one comes from the early days of the Roman Empire, and a game known as *pagancia*, which was played with a bent stick and a ball made from leather filled with feathers. The early golf balls were also made with feathers stuffed into leather covers. An early version of golf, perhaps?

The case against *pagancia* is that the ball is thought to have been at least 4in wide, which is rather different from the golf ball, although there are times when we all feel it would help our golf if it was.

With the expansion of the Roman Empire came a whole clutch of similar sports, particularly in France and the Low Countries – *cambuca* and *jeu de mail* were among them.

Enter exhibit two: *cambuca* was played in England during the 14th century where men propelled a ball towards a mark in the ground using a curved club. King Edward III, a killjoy if ever there was one, banned the game in 1363, telling the men to practise archery instead.

Jeu de mail, exhibit three, was played in Southern France and here the object was to hit a ball with a wooden club along a course, which was about a half-mile long, to a fixed point. The winner was the player who completed the course in the least number of strokes, which is, of course, a concept not unlike the one used in golf. Similarly, the ball was only 2in in diameter.

But exhibit four is the one that represents the greatest threat to Scottish claims, the Dutch game of *spel metten colve* (game played with a club), which was well established by the 13th century and the name evolved from colf to kolf.

The Scots like to point out that this was essentially an indoor game and that the balls were the size of cricket balls. However kolf also took the form of a cross-country game, played in a series of separate holes with implements that were not unlike early golf clubs and with wooden balls 2in in diameter. The ball was even teed up on a small cone of sand, just like the golfing practice at the start of the 20th century.

It is at this point that Scots' historians always play their ace card: show me the evidence that demonstrates that the Dutch used these clubs and hit these balls towards a hole – there is none. Indeed, early Flemish paintings showed participants playing to targets such as church doors.

If we accept the Scots' case, that the art of holing out is the all-important refinement which makes a game golf, then they win the argument that they invented the sport. It's probably fair enough.

◄◄ **In golf's early days, many courses were located in the centre of towns and villages.**

▶▶ **The Old Course at St Andrews, allegedly the 'Home of Golf'.**

The golfing revolution

The origins of golf are uncertain but both the Scots and the Dutch claim to have invented it.

What is not disputed is that golf, or a similar game, has been played for over five hundred years and while the origins of the sport will always be shrouded in mystery, it is a certainty that it was the Scots who gave the game to the world. They were its pioneers.

Golf was certainly being played in Scotland in the early 1400s. We know this because King James II was so concerned that the sport was interfering with archery practice that he banned it in the Scottish Act of Parliament of 1457.

The Scots took little notice. Indeed, golf is often blamed for Scotland's humiliating defeat at the hands of the English at the Battle of Flodden Field in 1513. The Scots' archers, you see, were little match for their counterparts.

Still the game could not be suppressed. Mary Queen of Scots was so hooked that she was back playing just a few days after the murder of her husband, Lord Darnley, in 1567.

What is extraordinary is that it would be nearly another 200 years before the sport's followers got their act together and developed an accepted set of rules. The oldest club in the world is generally thought to be the Gentleman Golfers of Leith, later to become, as they are now known, the Honourable Company of Edinburgh Golfers, whose home course in modern times is Muirfield.

The Society of St Andrews Golfers, later to be awarded the title Royal & Ancient by King William IV in 1834, came into being ten years later. These clubs were more places to drink claret and eat than to play golf. It is no coincidence that the trophy for the Open Championship is an 'auld' claret jug.

As the industrial and imperial expansion of the Victorian era brought prosperity for many, so the wealthy English started to visit Scotland for their holidays. There they discovered the game and brought it back with them and, although in Scotland

it was played by everyone, south of the border golf evolved as a gentleman's pursuit, and traits of this remain in the exclusivity and snobbery that still surrounds so many clubs today.

Not that you should think that Scotland is free of exclusivity and snobbery. Just try getting a game at Muirfield; there's more chance of a woman being accepted as a member of the R & A at St Andrews.

Westward Ho! in Devon is England's oldest links course, created in 1864 when Old Tom Morris from St Andrews came down to lay out the holes. And so the golfing revolution in Britain was under way. The advent of the guttie ball – made from the hardened sap of the tropical gutta percha tree, which became malleable when boiled – at about a quarter of the price of the old feathery ball, made golf more accessible to everyone. But what really gave impetus to the burgeoning development of the game was the expansion of the railways. Visit the great links courses

in Britain, and nearly all of them have, or did have, a railway line running very close by.

In 1880 there were 60 clubs in Great Britain. Thirty years on there were 387; now there are 2,500.

It wasn't just the English who were travelling; the Scots made their way across to America and brought their beloved sport with them. It was largely through their efforts that the game took a hold on the eastern seaboard of the United States at the turn of the 19th century.

They didn't just go to that great land either. A number of Scots were engaged in trading links with India and in 1829 established the Royal Calcutta Club, one of the oldest in the world.

So word spread. By 1900 there were a number of clubs in both Australia and South Africa. The oldest course in continental Europe is generally accepted to be that of Pau in south-west France, which was founded by British visitors in 1856.

▲ **In keeping with the early traditions of the game, Westward Ho, in Devon, is one of England's oldest and finest links courses.**

▲ **The Ryder Cup has developed into one of sport's great contests. Here the European team pose after their win in 1985.**

However, generally the game remained an exclusive preserve of indiginous gentlemen in most European countries. It wasn't until as recently as the 1980s, when Great Britain and Ireland's Ryder Cup team was augmented with the best of the Europeans, that interest began to spread.

Golf arrives in America

In America, there were no such inhibitions. John Reid, an expatriate Scot from Dunfermline, Fife, is generally considered to be the 'father of American golf'. On 14 November 1888, together with a group of friends, he formed the St Andrew's Golf Club, distinguished from its forebear by the use of the apostrophe. Others soon followed, including Shinnecock Hills, which in 1995, hosted the US Open on the occasion of its centenary. By the start of this century the game had taken a grip on the United States. It is one that remains to this day.

Recent history

There are a number of explanations as to why the game of golf expanded so rapidly in the last 20 years of the 20th century, thus mirroring the explosion in interest during the same period in the previous century.

A prime reason must be the efforts of the top professionals. The game was exceedingly lucky that a group of handsome and charismatic figures should all emerge at the same time – Ballesteros, Faldo, Norman and Langer, put the game on the front pages of newspapers and magazines that do not usually pay attention to the sport, while television brought it into the homes of millions.

Furthermore, the fact that three of them were Europeans helped to make a contest of that previously one-sided event, the Ryder Cup. In 1985, Europe won the match for the first time in 28 years and for the first time on American soil two years later.

The explosion of interest in continental Europe was remarkable. Countries such as France and Germany started to play the game in numbers that could not have even been dreamt of before. Young Swedes put posters of Ballesteros and Norman alongside the traditional skiers on their bedroom walls. Europe had been kissed on the lips for the first time by the sport, enjoyed the experience and wanted more.

◀◀ Golf is truly an international game. Sweden's Jesper Parnevik grew up in Stockholm, but he now competes on the USPGA Tour in America and lives in Florida.

Worldwide game

Golf also experienced something of a 20th-century boom in Asia. In Japan there were fewer than 30 clubs in 1945 but there are several hundred now, despite the fact that vast tracts of the country are patently unsuited to playing golf.

Japanese fascination with the game has reached obsessive levels. It is estimated that nine million people play golf, but such is the shortage of courses and land, that fewer than 15 per cent ever have the chance to play on a course. Instead, they set off for the driving range.

I remember playing at Wentworth a couple of years ago and watching a Japanese golfer drive impressively from each tee, but around the greens he was hopeless. For a while I couldn't understand how someone could be so good at one facet of the game and so clueless at another, but it eventually dawned on me that here was a member of that uniquely Japanese species known as the 'driving range golfer'.

It can be expensive to join a Japanese club costing twice the usual amount for an annual subscription. Many large Japanese companies have bought courses in other countries.

But all this does not explain why traditional golf-playing countries such as Britain and America took to the game with renewed vigour. Even when American professional golf was supposed to be on the decline, newcomers were still flocking to the sport.

▼ **Most Japanese golfers have never set foot on a golf course and have to settle for visits to the driving range instead.**

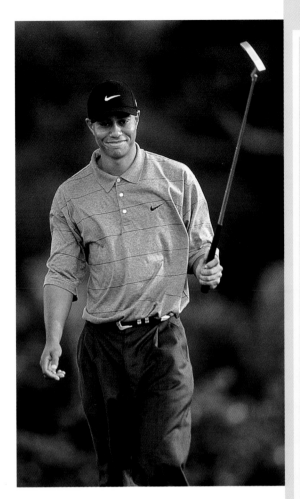

▸▸ Tiger Woods is undoubtedly the most famous member of the golfing elite at present. His talent and success have attracted fans from all walks of life.

My own theory is that, at a time when more traditional sports were embroiled in cheating and financial wrangles, the simple virtues of the game were emphasized. Europe's Ryder Cup victory at The Belfry came in the same year as the Heysel Stadium disaster in soccer. What would you rather do on a Saturday afternoon: go and watch a soccer game and worry whether a fight would break out, or play a round of golf? Thousands of people deserted the former for the safe refuge offered by the latter. In America a similar thing happened as fans of the traditional sports, such as baseball and football, were turned off by players already making millions and who were attempting to squeeze the games dry.

Suddenly the sport became fashionable. Big business enjoyed golf's clean image and poured money into it. In America, building companies quickly realized that a golf course was a considerable asset in persuading people to move to a particular property development.

The expansion of the game worldwide continues apace. In 1995, Volvo sponsored the first Chinese professional circuit, and one year later I played in the first Russian Open on the country's first 18-hole golf course on the outskirts of Moscow. On the practice ground, young Russians were practising their swings, just like young players anywhere else. The game has one language and clearly it speaks across all boundaries.

The Woods factor

One man, of course, is leading golf into a new age that will make it even more popular than ever. From Bangkok to Boston, Beijing to Buenos Aires, Tiger Woods is, to use modern parlance, 'the man'. Like Michael Jordan, his fame transcends the sporting arena and rivals the celebrity status of pop stars and actors.

Tiger first shot to international prominence following his first major tournament success – an amazing 12-shot victory in the Masters in 1997. The following US tour event was the Byron Nelson Classic, one of the US Tour's longest-running championships, where the previous record attendance had been a total of 150,000 people for five days. With Woods in tow the event became a 350,000 sell-out.

Woods has undoubtedly done much to make golf appeal to a younger and more socially diverse audience. He has also, most significantly, turned golf from a game that was much-maligned into a fashionable sport.

Quick fact

The volte-face that English journalist and television personality Michael Parkinson underwent rather summed up the changing attitudes to the sport. In 1975, as President of the Anti-Golf Society, the great raconteur amusingly wrote in *The Sunday Times*: 'There are now more golf clubs in the world than Gideon Bibles, more golf balls than missionaries, and if every golfer, male or female, were laid end to end, I for one would leave them there.' Some years later he had to resign. Yes, another convert had joined the flock.

Benefits of golf

A couple of years ago a marathon-running bore was given 1,000 words in a newspaper, which should have known better, to ridicule the so-called benefits of golf. And I suppose if your idea of fun is to pound up and down the pavements of this land for 20 miles or so each evening then yes, golf must seem sedate and calm in comparison.

The main thrust of his argument was that you'll never lose weight playing golf and you'll never get fit. As if the game was designed for either purpose!

One of the glories of golf is that people can continue to play it long after the marathon runner is hobbling at home on his worn out ankle and knee joints. The sport is a wonderful form of relaxation for the mind and the body as it gently massages both.

It is at this point that the marathon runner hits back, 'Relaxation my foot. I've seen these golfers who get all hot under the collar and turn puce when their ball disappears into a lake. How can that be a form of relaxation?'

▼ **The raw, natural beauty of a seaside links course can take your breath away.**

◀◀ Golf tournaments the world over now attract huge crowds when the top players compete.

Ah, but never forget that a little letting off of steam never did anyone any harm. And anyway, what is the first remedy that any doctor suggests to a stressed-out patient? It is certainly not to go on a 26-mile run. 'Go and play golf,' they'll say. And what is better than a game on a sun-kissed morning with the trees in full colour and the flowers in full bloom?

Perhaps the biggest benefit of the game is that it brings together so many like-minded people. Play golf with someone and you invariably find you have more in common than you thought. There cannot be a golfer alive who hasn't enlarged his circle of friends through the game. For this reason the sport has become a Mecca for businessmen. A round of golf with a client is seen as a valuable tool in attracting custom. Companies spend thousands of pounds on corporate golf days.

Many people even incorporate the sport into their holidays. When *Golf Monthly* magazine did a survey on the subject a few years ago, more than a third of its readers replied that they had taken a golf holiday abroad.

No, golf won't get you fit, and neither will you lose any weight, although the benefits of a five or six mile walk, which is what a round of golf entails, should not be ignored. Even so I'd say the number of benefits on each side works out as: marathon-running, two; golf, too many to mention.

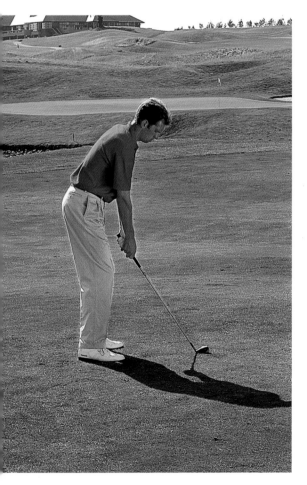

◀◀ Although best enjoyed in a group, golf is one of the few sports where you can play by yourself – and no-one else gets to see your bad shots, either!

Where to Play?

Of course, it was inevitable that, as the numbers who came into the game grew, so did the different ways available for them to enjoy their favourite sport. Now golf can be as expensive or as cheap as you want it to be. You can hit a bucket of balls on a driving range for next to nothing. Or, you can join the swishest of country clubs where you have to purchase a pricey debenture membership.

Options

No game has been more affected by new technology. Golf clubs and balls have been revolutionized, as we shall see in chapter three. Computer programmes now feature a huge selection of golf games and some of them are fairly realistic, or as realistic as you are going to get playing an outdoor game sitting in your armchair.

Computerized technology has also made it possible to play courses such as Pebble Beach in California without ever having to go there. These simulators portray each hole of the course in turn on a large screen. It tells you the length of the hole and how far the trees and the bunkers are from the tee. You then hit your shot at the screen and a computer 'reads' how far you have hit it and whether you have hit it straight or not. Some of them give very accurate readings as well. Of course it is hard to simulate a bunker shot and the green on which you will putt, which is usually situated in front of the screen, will be nothing like that at Pebble Beach. But on cold winter mornings this is an enjoyable way to keep in touch with the game.

Putting greens and pitch-and-putt courses are ideal for beginners or golfers who want to sharpen their short game. Most newcomers find they are clueless when it comes to chip shots and putts. Regular games on a decent putting green will prove absolutely invaluable once you start playing the game in earnest.

◀◀ Whatever the time of day, the practice putting green at a golf tournament is always a busy place.

Two groups of people inhabit driving ranges: the keen golfer who is desperate to cure a weakness in his game; and the raw beginner who is too scared to take his fledgling golf out on to the course.

Driving ranges can be boring and it is important not to just hit golf balls aimlessly. You will quickly lose confidence. Take your time and concentrate over each shot. All decent driving ranges have targets at 100yds, 150yds etc, so keep swapping and changing clubs and aim for the different targets. Set yourself challenges. Tell yourself you need to get this within 10yds for two putts for the Open – that sort of thing. Some people, once they have been bitten by the golf bug, install practice nets in their back garden, but here again it is important not to hit balls for the sake of it. Once you feel your concentration wavering, there is very little point in carrying on; take a break.

With the construction of so many new golf courses, one form of the game has really taken off in the last decade: the golf holiday. British Airways even has its own golf brochure now. There's hardly a developed place in the world you can't go and play golf for a week or two. Some places, like Myrtle Beach in South Carolina, have golf courses laid almost end to end. Some of them are terrific too, but then, given that there are some 80 to choose from over a 60-mile stretch, you would rather hope so, wouldn't you? Another branch of the game that has expanded rapidly is society golf. In fact the first society, Lloyd's of London, is more than 100 years old, but a myriad has sprung into existence in recent times.

However, the two most popular ways to play the game are at municipal golf clubs and by membership of a private club, and these are dealt with overleaf.

▼ The world's top golfers spend hour after hour on the practice range, refining their skills and grooving their swings.

Municipal golf

▲ **The famous Royal & Ancient clubhouse overlooks the first tee and the 18th green of the Old Course at St Andrews, Scotland.**

The local municipal is the place where the vast majority of people learn to play their golf. Some never leave. Some municipal courses are so good that you don't blame them.

Sadly, a few local authorities milk the municipal courses for all the money they can make, which can be a substantial amount. If you think that a municipal can cater for 100,000 rounds a year, then clearly if the money from all those round fees is poured back into the club, you should have a course and an establishment of which to be proud.

Unfortunately some local authorities reinvest just a fraction of the money they take in. At one course in Britain two summers ago, golfers were playing off mats in the middle of the summer because the tees didn't have a single blade of grass – a scandalous

state of affairs considering that the course has in excess of 80,000 visitors a year.

Of course there is a great deal of snobbery attached to golf and some people would rather give up the game than go near the local municipal. But the world's most famous golf course, the Old Course at St Andrews, is a municipal and there are many others up and down the country which offer a standard of play that bears favourable comparison with the private clubs in the area.

Municipal courses fell into disrepute during the golf boom at the turn of the 1990s. The stories were legion of people coming out of the pub on a Saturday night, parking their cars in the municipal car park and sleeping in the car in order to get a game on a Sunday. Most clubs have sorted out this nonsense now and operate an advance booking system.

Of course, patience is a word that most municipal golfers learn to have in abundance. Patience when the course is not of the standard they would like; mostly, patience with their fellow human beings, some of whom don't have the first clue with regard to the game's etiquette.

My advice for a complete beginner is to go to a driving range or a field and at least learn the rudiments of the game before progressing to municipal level. You will make life easier both on yourself and your fellow golfers.

A number of pay-as-you-play courses have sprung up around the country. Like municipals these are open for all golfers to play, the difference being that they are proprietor-owned and are generally in reasonable condition. They are usually more expensive too, although many offer value for money.

▼ The famous Brabazon golf course at The Belfry, in England, has been the scene of some monumental Ryder Cup matches in recent years.

Private clubs

▲ In total contrast to the accessibility of St Andrews, Augusta National – home of the Masters – is one of the world's most exclusive private clubs.

For some people, getting into the local private club far outweighs, say, a measly promotion at work. It is an ambition that dominates their life, and which can take years to achieve. It involves going before a selection committee and proving your suitability to be a member. If the club is a new one, then you might be lucky and get in straight away. If it is an established club, however, you had better brace yourself for a lengthy wait. Most clubs have membership lists of around 800 people and it really is a case of waiting until someone dies or moves out of the area and resigns his membership before a new member is admitted.

There are some clubs, such as Augusta National in Georgia, where you don't apply to be a member at

all. There they only have 300 members and only half that number actively play golf. It is simply a case of knowing a member and then when someone dies you may be invited to take his place. The price of joining Augusta is a well-guarded secret, but as for the annual subscription, the club just calculates its annual costs and then divides that sum by 300 and sends out the invoices.

Each year at the Masters at Augusta there is a party on the Saturday night of the tournament for the British press. It's a chance to meet some of the members, and no doubt you want to know if they are wealthy individuals. It is no surprise though that people are queuing up to join established golf clubs in Britain, as they represent an outstanding

◀◀ The spectacular and prestigous Pebble Beach links course has hosted several Major Championships, yet for most of the year it is open to the public.

◀◀ The Oxfordshire Golf Club, in England, is one of a number of American-style golf courses that were built in the UK in the 1990s.

bargain when compared to those overseas. Many clubs have reasonable annual subs and these become even more reasonable if you play at least once a week.

I remember playing Bamburgh Castle a gorgeous course in deepest Northumberland, where the annual subs as recently as 1998 were less than a weekend away. The members must feel like kids in a candy store every time they play.

But, you ask, aren't these private clubs bastions of male chauvinism? I'm afraid that many are. Some like Muirfield don't have any women members whatsoever; some merely tolerate their presence. At many clubs women are not allowed to play on Saturdays. This is obviously a throwback to the days

when women didn't have jobs, while it was one of the few days men could play. Maybe one day these clubs will leap straight from the 19th century into the new millennium.

Another irritation with private clubs is that they discourage the individual who loves to play different golf courses. The game is in danger of pricing these people out of the market. To play a championship course in the true sense of the word can cost a considerable amount of money. Even an ordinary private course will find you reaching far into your pocket, and if you visit in the winter months, you can find yourself on makeshift tees which are often in front of the ladies' tees. This is the kind of sharp practice that the sport can well do without.

Equipment

Golf clubs

▲ Jaime Ortiz Patino, owner of Valderrama, boasts an impressive and very valuable collection of golf antiques.

▶▶ Modern tournament professionals are hitting the ball further and straighter courtesy of the new technology.

History and memorabilia

How on earth could such a thing be worth such a lot of money? But old golf clubs have become an industry in themselves, with wealthy private collectors such as Jaime Ortiz Patino, the owner of the Valderrama course where the 1997 Ryder Cup was played, willing to pay astronomical sums for the game's most expensive memorabilia. In 1992, Patino paid near to a six-figure sum for a late-17th century rake iron. Even so, he is unable to get his hands on a lot of the best stuff. The clubhouse walls of the Honourable Company of Edinburgh Golfers at

The man from Sotheby's held the old club in his hands. He ran his fingers over the smooth shaft and stared at its long-nosed face. The club was more than 200 years old. He looked up and smiled and said, 'You're looking at a club here that could fetch a six-figure sum.'

Muirfield, and the Royal & Ancient Golf Club of St Andrews, for example, contain paintings worth millions of pounds.

The earliest golf clubs were often made by family carpentry or wood-turning businesses. By the mid-19th century the leading golfers were often the leading clubmakers as well, men such as Willie Park Snr, the winner of the first Open in 1860, and Old Tom Morris from St Andrews.

The long-nosed woods these men made, and which are of such value today, died out soon after the arrival of the guttie ball. Clubs became shorter, broader and deeper to cope with the fact the ball was harder and heavier. Then came the irons, which did not damage the guttie ball as they had the feathery.

By the time of the First World War all clubs were made with hickory shafts. But so many were being made that the supply of hickory was becoming scarce. Experiments with steel shafts began as early as the 1890s, but it wasn't until the 1920s that they were being freely used in the United States. In 1929, the R & A legalized them.

The age of mass production had begun and so did the practice of numbering clubs rather than naming them. Soon the driving cleek, the iron cleek, the lofter, and others became obsolete.

Steel lasted unchallenged until the 1980s. It is still the dominant shaft today, but in grave danger of being overtaken in the near future by graphite. As graphite challenged steel, so steel was edging out wood as the favourite material for the head. Oddly enough they're still called woods even though few people play with wooden-headed clubs today. A lot of the top players still favour wood, however. It is like the argument between CDs and vinyl. Like CDs with their clean sound, it is hard to argue against metal-headed woods, since they propel the ball further. But for some nothing beats the warm sound of the ball coming off the 'meat' of a wooden head.

Metal-headed woods were a liability in the early days with the advantage of greater distance being outweighed by the absence of accuracy. But rapid strides forward were made, and now you would have to belong to the Jurassic age not to play with one. The great advantage of metal woods is that they are so forgiving, which is a wonderful thing at club level but in the professional game I mourn the loss of the wooden heads. Shaping shots from the tee used to be an art accomplished only by the few; now players just stand on the tee and blast away.

In the last ten years metals such as titanium, and boron have entered the arena, for making both heads and shafts. Yet more exotica is promised from the boffins in the science laboratory in the future.

For me, it is something of a tragedy that the game's ruling body, the Royal & Ancient, has let all this technology come into the game without stepping in more firmly to protect the sport. In baseball, they still play with the same balls and bats as they did 60 years ago and so broken records are valid ones.

But can we really say the same about golf when someone like Tiger Woods breaks a course record using clubs that propel the ball 30yds further than the top players of even 25 years ago? And that's not counting the advantage given to him by improved golf balls.

Variety

Advances in technology mean that the golfer is faced with an almost bewildering choice of clubs today. It is not only the materials that are constantly changing. In recent years we have seen the introduction of six to nine woods, which do the job traditionally undertaken by mid-irons.

Many older players are thrilled with these new woods since they allow them to sweep the ball out of the rough, rather than cutting through the grass with an iron, thus compensating them for the power they have lost with advancing years.

As for the irons, the heads are either forged or cast. The traditional forged, or blade, iron is mostly favoured by good players, since it offers more feel at impact, and therefore enables them to impart more spin on the ball.

The majority of irons, though, are cast-iron and cavity-backed. They are peripherally weighted, so that the weight is spread around the whole face of the club and not concentrated on the 'sweetspot'. While this means that shots played with a cavity-backed club do not feel as satisfying when they come out of the middle of the club as they do with the blade, equally, they don't feel anywhere near as bad when the shot is mistimed. Miss-hit with a blade and the ball will go nowhere, leaving you with a stinging sensation in your fingers. But the cast-iron club is much more forgiving, and is thus favoured by all but single-figure handicap golfers. A beginner shouldn't consider playing with anything else.

Your first set of golf clubs will almost certainly have a textured, vulcanized rubber grip, perfect for use in all types of weather. Many top players are now reverting to a version of the traditional leather grip, again for more feel. It is not something with which average golfers need concern themselves; precise fine-tuning can wait until later.

As for the club shaft, the options are almost limitless. There's not just steel, boron, titanium or a pretty-coloured graphite from which to choose, there's a range of flexes from which to select as well. Not surprisingly, many raw recruits emerge from their first visit to the local professional's shop or golfing superstore baffled and totally bewildered. There are some useful hints overleaf as guidance when embarking on a journey through this particular labyrinth.

▼ The introduction of the metal wood has transformed golf, making the game easier and more enjoyable for golfers of all levels, particularly beginners and higher handicappers.

▼ Although manufacturer's would prefer that you bought their full range of fairway woods, there's nothing wrong with mixing and matching your clubs to suit your game.

◄◄ A set of golf clubs is usually comprised of nine different irons, but you can add to the range if you want an extra wedge or a long-iron.

◄◄ Unlike their predecessors, modern golf grips are designed to perform very well in all weather conditions – even heavy rain.

Best buys

◀◀ **Nick Price uses regular length golf clubs, but they will be custom-built to suit his swing characteristics.**

Buying a set of golf clubs is rather like buying a car: first you have to decide how much you want to spend. Then you have to remember that there's more than one model which is suitable for you. Of course you can spend a lot of money on a set that may well offer a smoother ride, but if you're a beginner are you really going to appreciate the difference?

My advice would be to start off with a set of game improvement clubs – all the main manufacturers have

a range. If your budget is tight you can begin with a half-set – especially if you're a junior and not sure whether you are really going to like the game.

Forget the graphite, the boron and the rest; a couple of metal-headed woods will be more than adequate to set you on your way.

Alternatively, if you are visiting one of the golfing superstores, don't forget to look at the range of second-hand clubs. However, avoid clubs where the grooves in the face have become worn down through too much use. Check the shafts for signs of stress and wear and tear and rust around the hosel. Also check the grips. When you hold the club the grips should live up to their name. Is the grip shiny? If it is, then it needs replacing.

Second-hand clubs, though, can represent a good investment if they are not too old, and particularly in the early days when you still have to decide if you are going to commit yourself to the sport. A quality set of second-hand clubs will serve you longer than a cheap set of new clubs.

If you're especially tall or short you should consider clubs that have a shaft that is either longer than standard, in the case of the former, or shorter for the latter. For anyone over 5ft 4in or under 6ft 2in, a regular shaft will suffice.

Finally, look after your clubs. Take a towel with you out on to the course and ensure that any mud or grass is cleaned from the face after any shot that has involved taking a divot. Always give them a rinse and wipe down after each round. The last thing you want is dirt coming between the face of the club and the ball at impact.

◀◀ Scottish golfer Gordon Sherry is almost 6ft 7in tall. He wouldn't be able to reach the ball using standard length clubs and therefore he has to play with a specially-built set.

Golf balls

History and development

If new technology has made a huge difference to golf clubs, it is nothing compared to what has happened with the development of the golf ball. In 100 years we have gone from balls that couldn't fly more than 100yds with a following wind, to ones that would travel five times that distance if the Royal & Ancient didn't impose strict controls.

Nevertheless, the improvements are vast even within the R & A's guidelines. Thirty years ago, if you bought a dozen golf balls, two invariably would not be perfectly round, and a couple more would cut after a few blows. Now you can guarantee that you will get 12 golf balls that all conform exactly to the manufacturer's specifications.

In the last five years further breakthroughs have been made. Now we have golf balls that have bypassed the tests, that both fly forever and land on a dime. Says professional Phil Mickelson: 'I used to go on a golf course usually believing that half the holes I could potentially birdie and half where I would be happy with a par. Now they are all potential birdie holes as far as I am concerned. It has made the game very exciting.'

Exciting for Mickelson, maybe, but the governing bodies are going to have to step in. The tests clearly need updating.

The first golf balls were almost certainly made of beech, before being replaced by the feathery ball early in the 17th century. These were arduous things

▲ The biggest technological advances in golf have involved the performance and durability of the ball.

▶▶ Even in the old days, golf ball manufacturers still experimented with their dimple patterns to make the ball fly further and straighter.

◀◀ The original golf balls took a long time to make, were expensive to buy and very easily damaged.

Competition intensified among the ball manufacturers. Others tried various patterns on the surface of the ball in an effort to make it fly further. Clearly, a ruling was needed to prevent matters getting out of hand and in 1921 the R & A decided on a uniform ball with a diameter of ¾in.

Ten years later, the United States Golf Association, the ruling body in America, increased that size to 1.68in. The two balls remained in the market place for over 60 years. The British size offered more control for the average player and more distance. The American size promoted more feel and was preferred by the better golfers. In 1987, the R & A decreed that the American size ball would become mandatory.

As the Haskell ball evolved so the patterns were replaced by dimples. Essentially it is the dimples that make the ball fly, as they minimize the effect of drag. Since dimples determine the ball's flight, the manufacturers are always playing around with their configuration in a quest for perfection.

Four years ago I visited the Wilson factory in Memphis, Tennessee, where they have balls for every circumstance and every player. They took me to the testing factory where all day a robot thrashes balls that exhibit different properties: balls that don't slice or hook; balls that would fly to the moon if you hit them hard enough; balls that don't fly 100yds even when struck by a top player. 'It's a shame we have to abide by the rules, isn't it?' quipped a spokesman. However, for once the laws seem sensible, as there isn't a golf course in the world that had sufficient protection against some of these wondrous missiles.

to make and even the most experienced manufacturer could make only four in a day. They were accordingly expensive to buy and were easily damaged. Even so, the feathery ball hung around for 200 years before the dramatic arrival of the gutta percha ball in 1848. For the first time, golf balls could be mass produced, bringing the cost down considerably, and this brought the game within the reach of far more people.

In turn, the gutta percha was replaced in 1900 by the rubber-core Haskell ball. With this invention, the game entered the 20th century. It was created by winding strands of rubber around a solid core, and it offered greater distance. It was invented by a wealthy American amateur golfer named Coburn Haskell and such was its impact that Sandy Herd used it to win the Open Championship in 1901.

Which balls to play

In America last year, I visited a golf superstore outside Augusta, Georgia, where the US Masters is held each spring. I was absolutely agog at all the different types of golf ball available, and decided to count them for myself. I gave up when I got to one hundred.

The choice is mind-boggling, and particularly confusing for the beginner to select a new ball, so here's a few ground rules to help clarify matters.

There are, essentially, three types of golf ball. There is a one-piece ball which is covered in a thermoplastic substance called Surlyn and which you will often find at driving ranges. It feels soft when you hit it and goes nowhere. It is usually the cheapest in a shop and with good reason. It is to be avoided for all but basic practice sessions.

The two-piece Surlyn ball is the most popular on the market. This, oh raw recruit, is the one for you. The skin is thick and is uncuttable unless you take to it with an axe. Because the skin is thick the player is unable to impart much spin on it, and so the ball flies further. All the long-distance balls that you will come across are made with a two-piece Surlyn cover.

The ball for the good player is now made from a variety of different materials, but what distinguishes it is its slender skin. It used to be that these balls did not travel anything like as far as the two piece Surlyn but remained attractive to the low handicapper and the professional because their thin cover allowed a player to impart spin, and therefore stop the ball quickly on the green. Now the technology is such that the ball travels almost as far as the distance ball but still comes to an abrupt halt. No wonder the pros are so excited; no wonder the rest of us are waiting for the authorities to act.

Golf balls are expensive items so a beginner should seriously consider buying lake balls, which generally sell at a fraction of the cost of a new ball. As the name implies these are balls that have been reclaimed from a watery grave and are perfectly acceptable while you are getting to grips with the game.

The famous 18th hole at The Belfry features an enormous lake that a player has to negotiate not only with a drive, but also with a second shot as well. A couple of years ago the lake was dredged for golf balls and thousands were recovered. A local charity did exceedingly well from the proceeds.

◀◀ There are currently over 1,000 legal golf balls on the market to choose from. It will take you a very long while to try them all.

◀◀ The lake ball industry is big business in golf the world over. And risky sometimes, too!

◀◀ Although most golf balls are painted white, some golfers prefer a brighter colour – normally because they are easier to find.

Clothing, shoes and rainwear

▲ The dress code in golf has changed drastically from the days when players ventured on to the course wearing a jacket and tie.

Twenty years ago a golfer's wardrobe was so bad that even the moths didn't want a taste. Perhaps the American comic Robin Williams summed it up best, 'Golf is the only game where a white man can dress like a black pimp and get away with it.'

Now just look at what has happened to us all – we've swapped comedians for couturiers. Now the range is not only a place were you go to hit golf balls but also to display the products the fashion designers bring out every season. And everyone, from Marks & Spencer to Armani, are after a slice of the action.

In the distant past, golfers used to travel to the links in their work clothes with their clubs tucked under their arms, but as interest in the

▶▶ Shoes for all seasons; most manufacturers now produce a winter and summer range of shoes with different sole options.

game grew, so did the demand for clothing tailored to the pastime.

The first golfing fashions were probably the ceremonial red jackets now worn by the captain of a club. They did have a more practical purpose at one stage, since they warned other users of links land that was not privately owned that there were golfers about. Through the centuries the attire has changed considerably and mostly for the better. The baggy plus fours that were standard dress in the early 1900s have given way to trousers made from all sorts of fabrics reflecting the different seasons.

Women have moved away from the full-length crinoline dresses and skirts which required a rubber band around the end of the garment to prevent the wind billowing it just as the ball was struck.

As the sport became fashionable in the 1980s, so it became inevitable that it would in turn attract the fashion experts. Their impact has been marked and some players are paid millions to endorse a company product or clothing range.

Clothes horses like Nick Faldo and Tiger Woods even have their own range of clothes. Payne Stewart,

the colourful American golfer who was so tragically killed in a plane crash in 1999, used to wear plus fours in the colours of teams in America's National Football League. This proved a clever ploy in 1989, when he was in contention to win his first major, the USPGA in Chicago, for on the final day, Stewart wore the colours of the Chicago Bears. Naturally he became the favourite of the locals and he later credited their support with helping him over the tense, final moments. Some people thought he looked idiotic. Stewart's reply was typically laconic. 'I get paid $300,000 a year to wear these clothes. Now who's the idiot?'

Most clubs have a dress code and denim items or T-shirts are all too often forbidden. Some clubs still insist on members wearing a jacket and tie in order to get a drink in the main lounge, but thankfully this practice is dying out.

A rainsuit and proper golf shoes are not supposed to be fashion items but are essential accessories that

▲ **Plus fours may be slowly dying out, but they are still an excellent way of keeping your trousers clean and dry when playing in miserable conditions.**

you will need. Some players like to play in golf shoes that have rubber soles, but most prefer those with spikes, which give you a better grip when playing a shot from a sidehill lie, or a bunker shot where you need a firm footing. It may seem an obvious point, but do make sure they fit properly – there is absolutely nothing worse than reaching the farthest point on a golf course and then discovering that your new golf shoes are crippling you.

Rainsuits have also improved immeasurably in recent years, with new lightweight fabrics that are designed not only to keep rain out but also to improve comfort while you swing the club without feeling inhibited. Before buying try on any item that interests you to make sure that you can swing freely, but be warned: rainsuits can be expensive.

Bags, tees and markers

It is not known when and where golf bags were invented. J. H. Taylor of Westward Ho! claimed they were invented locally by a retired sailor, who made some canvas bags to prevent the grips of the clubs from getting wet when it rained. However, some of the old

caddies didn't like the introduction of golf bags and in protest used to carry the bag under one arm and the clubs under the other. Contrast that with the lot of today's caddies, who can have as much as 35lbs slung over their backs, such is the volume of accessories carried on to the course by the top professional.

Many regular golfers have two golf bags. One is designed to be placed on a trolley and will be of sturdy construction with ample pocket space to carry the necessary accessories. The other will be a lightweight bag for those days when the trolley cannot be used owing to wet conditions, or simply when the player fancies carrying his own clubs. Make sure the zips are of good quality and not likely to break or seize up. Ensure as well that there is a full

◀◀ **The modern golf bag is lightweight, eye-catching and well-designed, not to mention easy to carry.**

hood that you can snap over the heads of the clubs when it is raining. Most golf bags have plenty of room to carry items other than the clubs.

And what are the necessary accessories? Golf balls, obviously. Tee pegs as well. These are either wooden or plastic and, as the name implies, for use only on the tee. You'll need a couple of ball markers to mark your ball on the green while you clean it before putting. A pitchmark repairer

enables you to repair any divots caused by the ball thudding into the green. A couple of towels are always useful: one to keep the grips dry in inclement weather; the other, which you can attach to your bag for ease of access, to clean your ball before putting and before driving off. You'll also need a couple of pencils for filling in the dreaded scorecard. Finally, an essential item when playing the game, particularly in Britain – a golf umbrella.

◄◄ **Tee pegs are essential for playing golf. Always make sure you have plenty in your bag before you head to the first tee.**

▲ **As well as up to 14 clubs, you'll need to pack a whole range of accessories into your golf bag before you play.**

Trolleys, gloves and headcovers

Among optional items is the golf trolley, which was first used in the United States in the early 1920s. Today, they have largely taken the place of the golf caddy. Most are lightweight and easily collapsible for practical storage.

Golf trolleys have also been greatly helped by new technology. Some are now computerized and by the simple press of a button will propel themselves down a fairway, leaving the player unencumbered with nothing more than a small remote control gadget to carry.

For many golfers, trolleys are an essential item since they take the strain out of carrying a full bag. Equally, many golfers can't stand the sight of them. They don't feel that they're playing proper golf unless the bag is slung over the shoulder. A glove is another accessory that is an

◄▲ Golf gloves help you grip the club more securely and come in a range of sizes and colours to suit your physique and personality.

◄◄ Tiger Woods would probably wear a cap when playing golf anyway, but Nike pay him several million dollars each year to make sure that it is their logo adorning his headgear.

essential item for some and optional for others.

Most players use one as it helps to keep a firm grip on the club. Remember, if you're a right-handed golfer you need a left-handed glove, since it is the left hand that grips the club. The glove should fit snugly: not so tight that the leather stitching is strained; not so loose that there's a spare half inch at the end of each finger. Some golfers, like Fred Couples, cannot see any use for them at all. It has probably cost him a million dollars in endorsements.

Headcovers used to be an essential item. When replacing an iron into a bag it would have been easy to hit a wood and damage it if a headcover was not in place. But with the advent of metal-headed woods, this is less the case now. Some players have covers for each iron as well, but don't bother with these unless you are the sort of person who has the patience to replace them after each shot.

As for headgear, a bobble hat is always useful in bad weather. You may get used to a visor or a cap on sunny days as well. Bear in mind, though, that most professional players use one of these items less for their usefulness and more because they offer a prime advertising spot.

▲ **Australian superstar golfer Greg Norman has his own range of branded golf clothing.**

The Basic Swing

▲ It's no coincidence that Tiger Woods, one of the longest hitters in the game, also has one of the most classical swings.

Develop your own Swing

Some of the great golfers had swings that made an orthodox player weep and which defied supposedly golden rules. Gary Player couldn't swing the club without knocking himself over – so much for perfect balance. Arnold Palmer attacked the ball as if it was threatening his life – so much for smooth rhythm. In his prime, Jack Nicklaus committed a cardinal sin – his right elbow refused to remain tucked against his side at the top of the backswing. The achievements of these three, who ruled over golf's record books for 40 years until Tiger Woods came along, should convince you there is room for an individualist swing.

The message, therefore, is clear; if something is working for you for heaven's sake don't go and change it because a magazine article tells you it is incorrect. Just go out and enjoy your golf and to hell with worrying whether it looks right or not.

What is important to grasp, though, is that there are fundamentals that, if implemented in your swing, will make you a more consistent golfer. If you are a raw recruit, then you are perfect material for the pages that follow – you haven't got into any bad habits that need to be swept away!

Lessons and videos

The first thing to do after reading this chapter is to book yourself half a dozen lessons with a local professional who has a good reputation for teaching. The Professional Golfers' Association conducted a survey a couple of years ago, asking golfers which was the number one source for getting tips and advice on how to play. The overwhelming answer was their friends, with books like this one and magazines second and professionals an extremely poor third.

1 Group lessons are an excellent way for youngsters to get an early taste for the game. They are also more cost-effective than individual lessons with a golf pro.

Friends, books, and magazines can only take you so far. There is no substitute for first-hand commentary from an expert. Most will give you a discount if you book a block of six lessons. If that is still outside your budget, then some of the larger golfing establishments do group lessons. Of course this is not as helpful as one-to-one sessions, but I'm prepared to bet that you'll learn far more than from your 16 handicap playing partner.

In recent years the game of golf has become obsessed by instruction. On television, a tournament leader's swing is broken down into segments and each analyzed for faults. It's as if there is only way to swing a club. There isn't.

2 Good communication between the pro and the pupil is one of the keys to accelerating the learning process in golf.

3 Golf lessons should be enjoyable for the pro and the pupil. You learn much more quickly when you are relaxed and having fun.

If you're a total beginner and a little apprehensive about going for a one-to-one with your local pro, then these group lessons may help you to make initial progress. The professional will video your swing and talk you through its strengths and weaknesses. The more you learn, the more you will be able to trawl through some of the rubbish that is written on the subject these days and sort out the wheat from the chaff.

One thing to remember; golf is perhaps the hardest of all sports to learn to play. In the early days, it is very easy to get discouraged as you duff the ball about 10yds off the tee and find a long iron an impossible club to use. Just persevere, the ball will eventually get airborne. However, don't book yourself a tee-time at St Andrews three months from the day that you first pick up a club. Improvement in golf comes in fractions.

The grip

Dear Reader, it is at this point, as you try to enact the following manoeuvres, that we are about to have a little falling out. There is no point trying to make light of the following: gripping a golf club for the first time is about as comfortable an experience as the first time you get behind the wheel of an automobile.

All that I can offer in consolation is that once you've stopped throwing this book around the room in frustration and have got used to it, then it will save you endless hours of irritation in the future.

Just don't try to cheat. Don't think you can get away with holding the golf club any old way: you can't. And if you think it's awkward now, then it's as nothing compared to trying later to cure an incorrect grip.

How hard should you be gripping a golf club? This is a matter of some debate, and there is much disagreement amongst coaches. Sam Snead, the great American pro and perhaps the greatest swinger of a golf club of all time, would tell his pupils to imagine they were holding a little dove in their hands. Most modern-day teachers, however, would recommend you grip it a little harder than that.

Basically, you have got some leeway here. Just don't grip the club so hard that it feels as if the grip is a dangling rope to which you are attached and if you let go you plunge into a vast ravine. And don't go to the other extreme and grip it so soft, that you end up imitating a wimpish handshake.

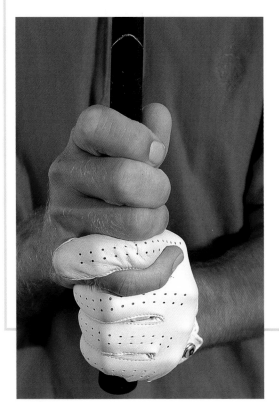

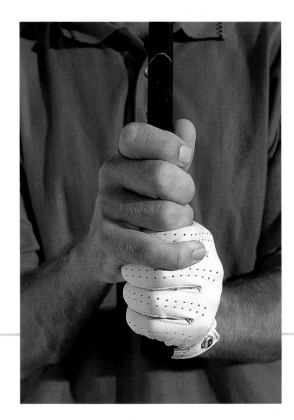

◀◀ The interlocking grip is ideal for players with small hands and short fingers. Jack Nicklaus and Tiger Woods both hold the club this way.

▶▶ The overlapping or 'Vardon' grip is the most commonly used among the world's top golfers.

Quick tip

One of the biggest destroyers of a good swing is a tight grip. Make sure that there is no tightness in your forearms when you hold the club.

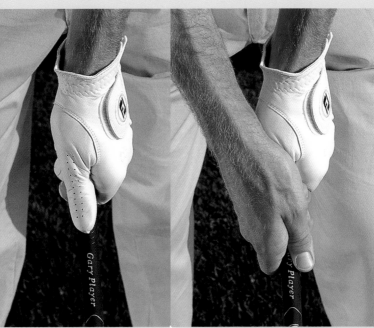

1 To create maximum power in your swing, hold the golf club more with your fingers than your palm. The grip should run from the knuckle joint on your left index finger to the base of your left index finger.

2 When you close your left hand around the club, position the thumb directly down the grip just right of centre. You should be able to see most of the logo on your glove when you look down at your grip.

3 When adding the right hand to the club, once again the grip should rest at the base of the fingers. Make sure that the lifeline on your right palm slots right on top of your left thumb.

Stance and posture

Golf may be a sport where you walk miles, but it is, in fact, played in inches and when everything is out of synch by inches, it can have a disastrous effect. That is why it is the hardest game. For example: position the ball in front of your left toe and you will hook the ball horrendously. Now bring it back three inches so that it is opposite your right heel, swing exactly the same and, aha!, it flies straight as a dye.

The stance is the easy bit. Stand with your feet parallel and shoulder width apart. Your right foot should be pointed slightly outwards. Your knees should be flexed a little. Stand up – don't crouch.

1 If you are unsure of what the correct posture should feel like or how far you should stand from the ball, stand upright and hold the club out in front of you horizontal to the ground.

2 Now flex your knees slightly, just enough to remove the tension from your legs but without causing you to lose any significant height.

3 Now tilt forwards from your hips, not your waist, to lower yourself to the ball. Keep your lower back nice and straight and allow your bottom to stick out a little.

Quick tip

Your posture should feel the same with each club, but inevitably the longer shaft of the driver means you will stand further away from the ball and more upright than when hitting the shorter-length pitching wedge where you will need to bend more to reach the ball.

For the wooden club shots, the ball should be positioned opposite your right heel, and for the irons, an inch or two further back. If you placed an iron club on the floor in front of your feet now, the club should be pointing exactly at the target.

How far should you stand from the ball? The hands should be away from the body, particularly with the long clubs, but the important thing is to feel comfortable and relaxed. Tension in the arm or leg muscles causes more bad shots than perhaps anything else.

Here's an easy tip to remember if you are not sure how far away to stand: grip the club and hold it out in front of you with your arms slightly flexed. Now bring it slowly down to the ground. When you reach the ground that is how far you should stand from the ball.

Backswing

The other day I was reading a book on the golf swing and the section on the backswing seemed to go on longer than *War and Peace*. At the end of it, the teacher offered seven checkpoints for the pupil to remember during the backswing. Seven! I would be surprised if anyone can remember seven checkpoints about anything during the second or so it takes to complete the backswing.

Here's a couple of good tips: keep your left elbow straight throughout, though not so rigid that it causes

1 Your address position is the key to your swing. Make sure that you are aiming correctly with a good posture and that for an iron the ball is played just forward of centre in your stance.

2 Swing the club away smoothly, making sure that your left arm remains relaxed and extended so that you can create a wide swing arc.

3 By the time you reach the halfway position in your backswing, your wrists should have hinged the club into a position where the shaft of the club is at 90 degrees to your forearms. See how solid the right knee is at this point.

Quick tip

Although a technically correct swing is obviously ideal, don't become too obsessed with positions. Good rhythm and tempo should still be the priority.

tension, and keep your right elbow tucked in adjacent to the side of your body. This will feel awkward at first, but try to remember these two things as you swing the club loosely back and forth. Try to get a feel for the rhythm of the swing and teach your muscles what is required.

On the backswing, your upper body will be rotating and your lower body will be resisting. Your eyes should not leave the ball. If all has gone well your shoulders will have turned 90 degrees and your hips half that amount. Your left knee will automatically be pointing towards the ball. If you are fit and agile, the club should be horizontal and pointing directly towards the target. If you're not, then take the club back as far as feels comfortable.

Be patient with the backswing. It is a most unnatural manoeuvre, but absolutely vital because the follow-through is a breeze if the backswing is properly compleddted. Good luck!

4 At the top of your backswing your hands should be nice and high, your right knee should not have moved much from its original position and your shoulders should have turned through at least 90 degrees.

The hitting area and follow-through

If the backswing is when you coil both your body and the club and imagine all sorts of exciting possibilities, then the follow-through is when you uncoil and realize all your potential. That's the theory anyway. Having got the backswing right, don't spoil it all by coming down from the top like a hurricane entering Miami Beach. Keep that right arm nicely straight.

Maintain your rhythm. Keep your eye on the ball. Let it all unfold naturally. It all sounds so easy doesn't it? Here's a couple of other things to digest. Make sure your body turns throughout and doesn't tilt. This is one of the most common faults in golf. It is caused because the player is so anxious to give the ball a helping hand that he leans back as he begins the

1 The transition between backswing and downswing is crucial. Many amateurs rush this part of the swing and this throws their timing out and leads to mis-hit shots. Start your downswing with your left knee and allow your hands to naturally drop down.

2 Coming into impact, it's important that you retain your height and keep your eye on the ball. Your body should continue to turn through as you swing your arms through the hitting area.

follow-through. The result is disastrous. Just practise that turning sensation in your living room. Feel your upper body turning to the right during the backswing and then back towards the centre during the first part of the follow-through, then your whole body turning towards the left during the second part. You should be perfectly balanced at the end, with your right toe pointing towards the ground. Grasp all that and the ball will go 200yds. But be prepared for a few hiccups along the way. Just remember two things:

1. Never get so discouraged that you feel like giving up.

2. Never get so encouraged that you think you're perfect.

Quick tip

No matter what kind of state your game is in, always commit to the shot and release the club. Trying to gently steer the ball down the fairway when you are lacking confidence rarely works.

3 Just as a top tennis player will rotate his forearms through the ball to hit a top-spin winner down the line, so a golfer must also release the clubface through impact to square the blade and produce power for the shot.

4 A balanced finish is a tell-tale sign of a good swing. Try to end up with most of your weight on the outside of your front foot and with just the toes on your right foot in contact with the ground. Hold your hands nice and high and finish with your chest pointing to the left of the target.

The Long Game

◀◀ **Mark Glynn is one of the world's longest drivers. Strength obviously plays a major part in hitting the ball a long way, but so does solid and consistent technique.**

The professionals think the long game is all a bit of an exercise in puffing out the chest and showing off a little. How else would the saying 'Drive for show, putt for dough' have come into being?

In a way they're right, of course. Long after he stopped winning tournaments people still flock to watch John Daly and it is not in admiration of his subtle touch around the greens.

People love to stand behind a tee and watch the top players drive off. It is this stroke more than any other that emphasizes the difference between the average player and the golfer he aspires to become. After all, a holed putt is within our reach. A bunker shot to 2ft we can hope to complete from time to time. A crisp five iron setting up a birdie putt is within the realms of possibility. But a 330yd drive is something we can only watch and admire, knowing that we can never match it.

For the newcomer to the game, of course, driving is not about showing off at all. It is about showing up without living in fear of making a fool of yourself on the first tee. Never mind 330yd drives, just let me hit it half that distance.

This section of the book is designed to help you keep your woods out of the trees. If you're a man, part of it is not about technique at all, but about keeping your macho tendencies in check. Quite what happens to men when they stand on a tee is probably something psychiatrists should study, but in the interim there is some advice that can be passed on to all golfing males.

Clearly the long game is about more than just standing on the tee and giving it your best shot with a driver. We will also take you through the fairway woods and the long irons that are invariably so troublesome to the average golfer.

What do you do when you're in a divot (after you've stopped bemoaning your luck, that is)? How do you cope with a downhill or sloping lie? How do you hit a deliberate hook when your natural shot is a fade? We shall answer all the questions that could conceivably be asked of your long game.

For the newcomer to the sport, then, the long game is not about puffing out the chest, but about conquering fear. The next time you stand at the back of the tee and watch Tiger Woods, David Duval, or Ernie Els, don't admire the flight of the ball and how far it travels, but study the things from which you can learn: the concentration, the rhythm, and the variety of clubs that a player will use to cope with the differing demands of each hole.

So forget fear. This chapter is all about enabling you to step on to the tee with a spring in your stride and confidence in your heart.

One to four woods

Of course, these days 'woods' are not made from wood at all. They're invariably made from metal and they make a ghastly sound when they meet the back of the ball. There are consolations: the ball goes further; the new generation of metal woods is very forgiving and so even a badly mishit shot will travel a fair distance.

As with the irons, the number of the wood indicates its potential with regard to how far the ball will travel. The lower the wood number, the less degree of loft on the clubface, the longer the shaft, and so the further you can hit the ball.

The driver or one wood, therefore, is the most powerful club in a golfer's armoury. Phil Mickelson regularly propels the ball 350yds with his driver. An average player will hit it about 220yds, but many amateurs, however, find it one of the most difficult clubs to use. It is the straight face that causes the problems. A typical driver will possess a loft angle of just ten degrees. Many are intimidated by it, believing that they will never get the ball airborne, so they try to help the process along, usually with fatal consequences.

Best, then, to start with a two or three wood, which is more helpful to the beginner. The former is basically a substitute driver and so really only suitable for use off a tee. The latter is a much more versatile club and the 15-degree loft allows a player to use it if the ball is lying in a good position on the fairway.

1 Because of the lack of loft on the face of a driver, you need to place the ball on a tee peg and play it forward in your stance to get it airborne.

2 The driver is the least forgiving club in the bag. Focus on keeping your swing as smooth and controlled as possible throughout.

3 At the top of the backswing, the shaft of your driver should be horizontal to the ground and aiming squarely to your intended target.

The four wood is an even more friendly piece of equipment but its 18 degree loft means you start to lose distance. It is ideal, though, for tee shots to narrow fairways, or fairway blows where the lie is none too favourable. You will even be able to use it in some instances in the rough.

The three wood is the one that you really do need to make friends with. Most players find that they have far greater accuracy with it than the driver and the loss of 15–20yds is, for the most part, inconsequential if you're on the fairway eight times out of ten instead of just two or three. Armed with this sort of philosophy, the Australian Peter Thomson once won the Open at Royal Birkdale without ever taking the driver out of his bag.

4 It is vital that you stay behind the ball through impact so that the clubface can sweep the ball off the tee with a shallow angle of attack. Keep your head behind the ball. Don't lunge with your shoulders.

5 The length of the driver and the momentum of your swing will pull you round into a full finish position. Always finish with your weight on your front foot and your right shoulder nearest the target.

Quick fact

All sorts of long driving records have been claimed over the years, but the different weather conditions in which they have been achieved makes it all a haphazard business and a bit of harmless nonsense. Perhaps the unluckiest longest drive, however, belonged to Carl Hooper who hooked his drive on the 456yds third hole at San Antonio Country Club during the 1992 Texas Open. The ball pitched on a cart path. It pitched again on the cart path. In fact it appeared to be drawn to the thing like a magnet and didn't stop rolling until it collided with a fence – a matter of 787yds from the tee. It took Hooper two full four-irons and an eight-iron simply to make the green. He took a double bogey and went on to miss the halfway cut by one.

Five to nine woods

Many players become very attached to their three and four woods. The same players detest their three and four irons. Why take a long iron when you can sweep away with a fairway wood, they argue. Make a mess with a fairway iron and it goes about 40yds, but botch up with a fairway wood and you can generally still scuttle the ball most of the length you had intended.

▶▶ Knowing that the average amateur hates using long-irons, manufacturers have developed a wide range of metal woods, starting from a driver all the way through to an 11 wood.

◀◀ Ireland's Christy O'Connor was known as a magician with a fairway wood in his hands and could play all kinds of wonderful shots with these clubs.

The manufacturers, being good listeners, paid heed to this argument. So they brought out a five wood which sits in nicely between a four and five iron. And that went down very well with the average player, who added that club and removed another iron from his bag.

As a player gets older the irons do become harder to use, particularly in the rough. The head of the club becomes entangled with the grass and it takes a certain amount of arm strength to keep the club on its intended flight path (sometimes the rough is so thick, of course, that it is almost impossible to keep an iron on its intended flight path).

Given this line of thinking, what followed next was perhaps inevitable: a range of woods to replace all but the short irons. Many older players now only carry an eight iron upwards. Many have more woods in their bags than irons.

First there was the six wood and then manufacturers like Callaway went the whole hog and made a range up to and including an eleven wood. There is something odd about watching a player take out, say, a seven wood for a shot of 140yds, but if it works who am I to knock it?

And if you're a splendid wood player, but lousy with the medium irons, even allowing for the vagaries in form and confidence and having practised hard, then do pop into your local shop and by all means

satisfy your curiosity and try them out.

For newcomers, it is best to tread a more conventional path at first. The laws of the game mean that you can only carry 14 clubs in your bag at any one time. Nine of them should be irons, or ten if you count a putter. That allows you plenty of scope with your woods and certainly a five wood is a very useful club to have in your bag.

▶▶ **The new breed of super drivers can add yards to your tee shots and they can also keep them straighter, too.**

Quick tip

When choosing your woods, do not be afraid to mix and match. You might like the three wood from one set, but if you don't like the look of the driver, then seek elsewhere. Every large golf shop will offer a healthy selection of individual woods, particularly drivers. It may cost you more, but isn't it worth it for the sake of your peace of mind?

Long irons

If there are two words that are guaranteed to induce ·a long face from the average player they must be 'long irons'. I mentioned in the introduction that no shot emphasizes more the difference between Joe Professional and Joe Average than the driver, but the contrast in confidence when using the long irons must run it close.

Take the following scenario: a nasty par four with water running in front of the green. The shot you have left calls for a four iron. What do you do? The professional hits a four iron. The amateur frantically racks the brain, trying to think of anything that will avoid using the four iron. Play short with a nine iron even. More likely, go with a wood and hit it 'soft', as they say.

There's no disguising that the one and two irons are the hardest clubs in the bag to use. The loft on a one iron is slightly less than a three wood and a two iron is the equivalent of a four wood, but the margin for error with an iron is much greater than with a wood. They're strictly for low-handicap amateurs and professionals only.

But come down to the three or four irons, with their greater loft, and here we have clubs that are within the bounds of most players. Practice is the name of the game here. You need to spend some time just hitting three and four irons to develop the confidence to use them when you go out on to the golf course.

The five and six irons, meanwhile, should be among the most accurate clubs in your bag.

▶▶ **Despite the advances in golf manufacturing technology, the long irons remain the most difficult clubs in the bag to master. Be prepared to put in plenty of practice if you want to hit them like the pros.**

As far as accurate hitting with irons goes, the play of two-handicap Bob Taylor in the 1974 Eastern Counties Foursomes Championship at Hunstanton takes some beating. In practice to the 188yds 16th hole he holed out in one with a one iron. Come the first round of the competition he repeated the feat, only this time with a six iron since the wind had stopped blowing. When he stepped on to the tee in the second round you can imagine how he was feeling. 'I'll offer you odds of one million to one against doing it again,' his partner jokingly remarked. Taylor took out his six iron – and holed again. Suffice to say that the real odds against that happening were many times more than one million to one.

◀◀ Professional players like John Daly have no fear of long irons.

Different tees

Clearly, some shots that you play on a hole are more important than others. A lay-up shot short of water, for example, allows you a fair margin of error. A four iron over water to a small green allows you little at all.

The tee shot is among the most important. It is by no means going to guarantee success on a hole, but it can confirm failure.

The first thing to appreciate is that their are many different teeing grounds available. Generally a course will offer three different tees: the one that stretches out the hole to its fullest length is usually indicated by a white post or marker and is the medal or championship tee; the middle one is invariably the tee of the day and here the colour is yellow; the red tee is for women.

In recent years this system has become more sophisticated and many courses now offer a greater variety of tees. At the Warwickshire in the English Midlands, for example, they offer 242 tees spread over the 36 holes and, by prior arrangement, you can play 18 holes stretching anything from 5,800yds to 7,400yds.

◀◀ Invariably the white (championship) tees add considerable yardage to the hole in comparison to the yellow (regular) tees. However on shorter holes the challenge will be similar for all abilities and genders.

What is vital is to play a course that suits your abilities. Generally the tee of the day will suit you fine. A course measuring 5,800–6,500yds is ideal. Only golfers with a handicap of 12 or under should be playing anything longer. Don't get caught up in any macho bravado. If you're playing a championship course, don't try to play off the same tees as the professionals. A 7,000yds course is no fun to anyone over a five handicap. You'll just find yourself having to play a succession of shots with your metal woods.

▼ **Playing from the competition tee (white) significantly increases the yardage and complexity of a hole, compared with the yellow (men's) and red (women's) tees.**

Playing from the tee

Before you play your tee shot take a moment to weigh up the hole's character. Visualize the shot you want to play and what you hope to leave yourself with for your second stroke. If a long drive will leave you with a wedge to the green and you are currently not speaking to your wedge, then take a three wood and leave yourself an eight iron.

Once you've decided on the shot you want to make and the correct line, find something on the hole or the skyline at which to aim and set yourself up accordingly. It may even be the flag itself, but it is crucial to have something upon which to focus.

Setting an intermediate target will help you deal with any intimidating factors such as deep fairway bunkers or trees on either side. Block out these features and concentrate on the object that you have decided to aim at.

To help him line-up, Jack Nicklaus, one of the great drivers of all time, would look at the ball, then a spot 18ins in front of it, then the place down the fairway where he hoped his ball would finish, and draw an imaginary line along all three. If he felt the line was at all crooked, he would adjust accordingly. It's got to be worth a try if it was good enough for the greatest golfer of all.

◀◀ The game's greatest ever player, Jack Nicklaus, never hits a tee shot without first carefully selecting his target and then aiming the club accordingly.

▶▶ Tiger Woods may be one of the most accurate drivers around, but even he will hit an iron off the tee when playing to a narrow fairway.

Quick tip

We're all guilty of it. You're playing in a personable four ball match and you're chatting away from the moment you leave the previous green to the moment you tee it up on the next hole. You haven't a thought in your head as you swish away at the ball and it finishes in trouble. There's an easy way to avoid this. Just give yourself a moment as you step on to the tee to work out exactly what you are trying to do. You don't have to be slow about it, but getting a picture in your mind's eye of what you want to achieve is vital to success. And after you've done it, you can chat away again to your heart's content.

Playing smart & fairway woods

It's a failing of many players that during a round they will just use one club off the tee for the 14 or so holes that are par fours or fives. Here's the way they think: a 500yd hole with two deep bunkers that narrow the fairway to just 20yds in width at about the distance you hit a one wood? Must call for a driver.

A 320yd hole with a narrow sliver of fairway at which to aim, owing to water down the left-hand side and trees on the right? Must call for a driver.

It is interesting to note that the straightest drivers of all such as Colin Montgomerie or Lee Westwood wouldn't dream of using the club in either of these instances unless there were three holes to play and they needed three birdies. Even given that situation, they would probably still use other clubs.

Many golfers fall back upon the argument that they are just having a fun round and using a three wood on one hole and a three iron on another would go against the grain. Which is fine, of course, but tell me about the really fun rounds that you have enjoyed: were you not playing well? Were you not scoring well? Most golfers would answer in the affirmative to both these questions, but taking a

◀◀ **Colin Montgomerie is known as one of the world's straightest drivers, yet even he will take an iron off the tee rather than risk hitting the ball into trouble with his driver.**

If ever a shot cried out for more thought off the tee it was Greg Norman's drive to the 18th at Royal Troon in 1990 in the four hole play-off for the Open Championship. Norman had started the play-off with two straight birdies and was in the, er, driving seat. At the 18th, he took on a bunker that was lying 320 yards from the tee to the right of the fairway and lost. He finished in it and never completed the hole. Another major championship blown.

▲ A simple case of poor course management when under pressure cost Greg Norman a chance of winning the 1989 Open Championship, at Troon, in Scotland (see 'Quick fact', right).

driver on every hole helps them achieve neither. Indeed, driving into the water or into the trees can have just the opposite effect as your score goes haywire and your confidence down the drain.

So think about it; if the fairway's narrow at the driving distance, don't look upon it as an irresistible temptation, but concede a small defeat to the course and use your three wood in the knowledge that you'll have a much better chance of winning a far greater victory by enjoying success on the hole. Or use your four wood if you prefer or if you think the situation calls for it.

▲ Taking the time to read the greens is a simple way in which you can improve your course management.

Using an iron from the tee

Another instance that shows up the difference between the way professional and amateur golfers think is in the use of an iron off the tee. Most pros consider it an essential part of their armoury to have a long iron that they can reliably use off the tee to find the fairway. Most amateurs use one off the tee only when it is required on a short hole.

One problem with long irons is that they require practice and technique, and most amateurs haven't got the time to be proficient in both of these categories.

But here's a little scenario: the first par three you play is 170yds and you strike a four iron beautifully into the heart of the green. The second par three is 190yds, downwind, and so you take another four iron and again you strike it well. The next hole is a short par four and the trouble is such it requires another 170yd tee shot. What should you do now? What

▼ **Using a long-iron (A) off the tee instead of a driver (B) is often a sensible strategy, particularly on a short par-4 hole.**

most professionals would do is take out a four iron. However, even when the logic of taking this iron is staring them in the face most amateurs would still prefer to hit a 'soft' fairway wood.

Here the problem is clearly a mental one. You've hit two perfectly acceptable four iron shots to short holes. Why not use the same club when there is a much bigger target to find, namely the invariably broader expanse of the fairway?

Conquering the mental barrier of using an iron in these circumstances and finding one in which you have confidence – be it a two, three, or four iron – is one of the keys to scoring well.

There may be nothing like hitting a wood as straight as an arrow, but equally there's nothing more sure to wreck a scorecard than gambling with a driver and losing. Going for glory all too often results in embarrassment and disaster.

Fairway wood or iron?

So you're in the middle of the fairway, you've got a smashing lie, and the green is 200yds away. What do you do now?

What you don't do is what eight out of ten amateurs do: dash back to your bag and wrench the cover off the three wood as fast as you can.

All right, I understand. Glory is flashing before your eyes. You can't see your ball in the water hazard on the left. There's no chance at all of your finishing in the bunker on the right. The only shot you can visualize is one that flies straight and true, finishing 20ft from the hole and your knocking in the resultant putt for a birdie three.

Now, before you take that three wood, answer this question: how many times do you complete that perfect stroke, particularly when inhibiting factors are present and the green is so well protected?

Most players are delighted if they hit the perfect shot once in 20 occasions. On the other 19 they either lose their ball in the lake or are confronted by a nasty sand shot. Here is a far better strategy. Take an iron or a smaller wood, so as to leave yourself a 20yd shot to the green. That way you take out of play both the hazard and the bunker. Admittedly, you won't get a birdie three. But you will get a four or, at worst, a bogey five, which is certainly better than the score you would be looking at if you were staring forlornly at your ball in the water.

There are times, though, when a three or four wood is a perfectly good option. If, for example, you are three down with four to play and your opponent is already on the putting surface in two, then clearly you have no choice. Dire circumstances call for drastic measures.

Maybe the entrance to the green is wide open, or you think you could give Ernie Els a game out of the sand. In those circumstances, by all means go ahead and blaze away.

The key is to let the stars clear from your eyes and then assess the shot in a calculating manner. If the penalties for straying off-line around the green are great, then go with an iron. Don't risk leaving yourself a shot you dread. Above all don't throw careless shots away by finishing in a lake.

1 Unless you are a very good player and strike your irons consistently, this is a dangerous pin to attack. The landing area is tiny, while sand and water await the mis-timed shot.

2 Golf course designers aren't totally sadistic. Most will include a bail out area that you can aim at if you don't feel confident enough to take on the very difficult approach or tee shot.

Quick fact

At the 1935 Masters, Gene Sarazen needed to play the last four holes in three under par to beat Craig Wood. At the par five 15th, his drive left him 220yds away from the green, with a lake protecting the front of the putting surface. Sarazen decided to take on the 'death or glory' shot. He struck a four wood as hard as he could. The ball pitched on the front of the green, hopped on and on before finishing in the hole for that rarest of birds, an albatross. Sarazen went on to win the title. His miraculous blow helped publicize the tournament, which was then in just its second year, and became known as the 'shot heard round the world'.

Uphill and downhill lies

In a dream round of golf, every tee shot flies down the middle and every approach is played from a perfect lie on the fairway. So much for fantasy golf; now for reality. Even when you hit the ideal drive, you might find yourself in a difficult lie for your second shot.

An uphill lie shouldn't cause you too many problems. The things to remember are to swing as normally as possible and to take a club higher than is usual, or two more if the gradient is severe. This is because the uphill lie will automatically cause the ball

1 From a downslope, set your weight more towards your front foot and play the ball back in the stance to guarantee good contact.

2 The lie of the land will cause you to make a slightly steeper backswing than normal. This is not a problem.

3 Allow your weight to go with the shot through impact. You shouldn't have too many problems getting your weight across onto your front foot.

Quick tip

When playing from a downhill lie to the green, remember to aim some 10yds to the left of your intended target. A downhill lie distorts the plane of your swing, so even a perfectly struck shot will fade away to the right.

1 From an uphill lie the ball will will fly higher than normal, so take a less lofted club than normal for the shot and set your hands ahead of the ball.

2 Although you may find it difficult to achieve if the slope is particularly severe, you should try to finish with your weight on your front foot.

to fly up more than usual, with consequent loss of distance. If you are playing into a strong wind, the loss will be quite dramatic, so place your hands ahead of the club at address to help compensate.

At address most of your weight will fall naturally on to the back foot and your front knee will buckle, but the most important thing is to be careful not to lose your balance on the backswing.

The downhill lie causes far more errors. It is a scenario that an amateur player will perhaps

encounter only once every other round, and such unfamiliarity causes fear. Many people hit behind the ball as worries over the gradient's effect causes them to lose their balance and rhythm and to lift their head too soon.

A good tip is to move the ball back an inch in your stance. Because your weight will naturally be on the front foot, it is vital to concentrate on retaining your balance. Swing slower than normal and take a more lofted club to get your usual trajectory on the ball.

Ball below the feet and above the feet

In these two situations, the flight of the ball will be considerably affected. Side-spin will be applied in both cases, causing the ball to hook if it is above your feet and slice if it is below.

Here again it is important to swing normally and to retain your balance and rhythm. Don't try to fight the ball's natural inclination to deviate from the straight and narrow, just make allowances.

1 When the ball is above the level of your feet, choke down on the grip and stand taller than normal to allow for the fact that the ball is nearer to you than normal.

2 When the ball is below the level of your feet, tilt forward more from your hips, grip the club at the end and increase your knee flex to lower your body.

Quick tip ⏱

If you are used to playing your golf on parkland courses and are planning a first trip to the great links venues, then it would be wise to practise a few shots from sloping lies before you go. Only Birkdale and Muirfield have predominantly flat fairways. Some of the others, like Sandwich and Turnberry, leave you with shots that will offer plenty of food for thought!

When the ball is above your feet, your hands have to be placed further down the grip. If the slope is gentle, then an inch or two will do the trick, but if it is severe then you may have to go down to the very bottom of the grip.

The ball will hook because the awkward set-up position causes your swing to be much flatter than usual. Lean forward slightly so that your weight is more towards your toes.

When the ball is below your feet all the opposites apply. The swing is more upright and so the ball will slice away to the right. Keep the weight towards your heels to help maintain your rhythm. Grip the club slightly further up the shaft than normal, but not so

▲ **The rugged and undulating terrain of many links golf courses means that you will rarely find a dead flat lie – even in the centre of the fairway.**

far that the heel of your left hand is hanging off the end. Flex the knees a little more.

Because the slice of the ball will cause you to lose distance, you may want to take at least one club more in these circumstances. The extra length in the shaft of the longer iron will help you to retain your balance and so avoid the all-too-alluring temptation to force the shot.

Playing from a divot

Is there really anything more maddening in golf than hitting a drive that splits the fairway in two, you're walking after it, congratulating yourself on your efforts, and then you find your ball has come to rest in a divot? Do you look up to the heavens and sarcastically offer your thanks? Do you launch into the golfer's lament of misfortune (Harry Vardon, way back in the early 1900s, made the wry comment that he had never come across a fellow who considered himself lucky on the golf course)?

1 Playing from a divot shouldn't cause you too many problems. All that's required at address is slightly more knee flex to help lower the base point of your swing.

2 Most top players abbreviate their backswing slightly when hitting from a divot because of the 'punch' style action through the ball required to get it moving forwards.

3 Make sure that your hands lead the clubface through impact so that the clubface squeezes the ball out of the divot. Expect the ball to fly further than normal because of the lack of backspin.

I suppose finding yourself in a bunker is worse in some respects, but at least you've hit a bad shot to end up there in the first place, but come now, pull yourself together. Finishing in a divot is very annoying because of the blatant unfairness of it all, but it is nowhere near as fatal as finishing in a footprint in a bunker. There you're almost certain to drop a shot at the very least. In a divot, you'll just lose a little control, but not so much that you should miss the green.

Although the ball is sitting down more than is usual, don't go digging after it as though you're after buried treasure. Flex the knees a little more and otherwise swing normally. Accept that you are not going to be able to hit the bottom of the ball and so impart spin.

It will run about 20yds further than normal, so take a club less than is usual. Other than that, no problems. What's all the fuss about? What's that . . . your ball has finished in a divot and your next shot requires a high seven-iron over the water to a small target? In that case, look up to the heavens, sarcastically offering your gratitude.

The Short Game

▲ The ability to pitch the ball close to the hole from within 100yds of the green is invaluable. It is an area where the top golfers really excel because it enables them to make birdies on short par fours and long par fives.

▶▶ Gary Player is known as the game's ultimate bunker player. When once told by a spectator that he was lucky to hole a shot from the sand he replied: 'The harder I practise the luckier I get.'

It seems perverse that, if a 400yd par four is played correctly, a player will take only two shots to cover 394yds and then two more to cover the last six. Even when played less accurately for a five, it is odds-on that a player will take two shots to cover 390yds and three to cover the final ten.

In this section we will concentrate on all those important shots that come in the last few yards of each hole. If your driving and long iron play make you want to stick out your chest and feel smug, then the time to get serious, and where you can really save yourself a lot of strokes, is with the short irons. This is where you make or break your score. After all, it doesn't matter how much you improve, unless you have super-human strength, you will never be able to cover 394yds in anything better than two strokes; however, confidence in your chipping, pitching and putting will help you turn three shots into two and even two into one.

We will analyze all shots from 150yds in to help you improve. In particular we'll concentrate on the shots that cause acute problems to most beginners: the bunker shot from a compacted lie; the pitch shot from a bare lie over a bunker; the shot over a stretch of water. Yes, I know, it sends a shiver down the spine merely thinking of them, but we'll help soothe your doubts and fears.

Here we come on to the key factor regarding the short game: the importance of confidence. You'll have often heard it said that golf, like many major sports, is mostly played in the mind. The short game is 90 per cent played in the head. It is primarily about confidence. But to have confidence you have to have the correct technique to play each shot and then you have to practise that technique until it becomes second nature. The great thing about practising your short game is that you don't need acres of land in which to do it. You can practise your chipping in your back garden. You can practise your putting stroke on the carpet at home.

Therefore don't worry about not having the time. Ten minutes every other evening just chipping a few

balls will make an enormous difference when you come to play your golf.

Of course practising a pitch shot over water is a little difficult, unless you've got a swish mansion with a stream running through a three-tier garden. But it's surprising, once you have grasped the principles regarding the short chips and pitches, how the fears you had regarding those of 40yds or so also fall away.

Putting is a game in itself – the game within a game – and it doesn't matter how good you become, or how confident you feel going to the course, you will still have days when you couldn't hole a putt if your life depended on it. So I'm afraid the bad news is that those days never completely disappear, no matter how good you become.

We will show you how to ensure good days as well, though, days when God is clearly in his heaven and you will feel the Chosen One and that you can't do a thing wrong on the greens.

Putting is the great equalizer: it's the one area of the game where all players, be they professionals or humble amateurs, look much the same. This is where you can see the importance of confidence: if a professional holes a 10ft putt to break an unlucky streak, you can almost guarantee that they'll hole another shortly after. Something has slotted into place and whatever that something is, it invariably comes back to confidence.

But confidence is much easier to talk about than to acquire: in golf it is a quality borne of good technique and long hours of perseverance. This book will show you how to acquire the technique. It will also demonstrate that perseverance doesn't have to be one of the most boring words in the English language.

Seven iron to wedge

The short irons comprise those clubs from the seven iron down through to the wedge. The higher the club number, the shorter the shot and the greater the need for accuracy. Any reasonably proficient player will be hoping to hit the green at least eight times out of ten with any clubs numbered seven, eight or nine. Any professional will be truly disgusted if he doesn't get the ball within 20ft with a wedge.

Most beginners start out hitting shots with clubs such as the seven iron and quickly make friends with

1 When hitting a wedge shot, make sure that your stance is fairly narrow. It is perfectly acceptable to aim your feet a fraction left of the target to give yourself room to swing the club through impact.

2 The shorter length of the shaft means that it is unlikely that you will be able to reach the horizontal with a pitching wedge. But when accuracy is more important than power, there is no need.

3 Just because you are playing a fairly short-range shot, it doesn't mean you should swing slowly through the ball. Swing at your normal speed and commit fully to releasing the club, just as you would with a long-iron.

them. The natural loft of the club means that they are straightforward to use and there is no problem getting the ball airborne. The accent is on finesse and accuracy and the vast majority of players feel more comfortable trying to transmit those qualities with a golf club than when the accent is on power.

The maximum distance we are talking about here is 150yds, about the outer limit that a good player will expect to hit a seven iron. More typically, the average amateur will hit it 130–140yds, and because it is so important that you hit the greens frequently with these clubs, it is vital you know just how far you hit your seven iron. It is a simple thing to discover. Go to the nearest patch of land and pace off 150yds from your bag, placing an umbrella in the ground. Now hit 20 seven-iron shots to the umbrella and note the range between your best and worst.

If most of the balls have gathered in a cluster or gone about the same distance, then clearly that is how far you can hit a seven iron. But don't fall into the web that traps so many players: one of the 20 balls has reached the umbrella and so the next time the player has a 150yd shot to a green he takes a seven iron, thrashes it to death, and wonders why he hits it badly, finishing 15yds short. Sheer folly! Once you know your capabilities with a seven iron, take 10yds off for each club of a higher denomination.

4 Many amateur golfers allow their weight to fall onto their back foot through impact in an attempt to scoop the ball into the air. Let the loft on the clubface do the work and make sure that you finish with your weight on your front foot.

Quick tip

Always remember that you can save many more shots practising your short game than with your long irons or driver. If your practice time is limited and you don't know whether to work on your ball striking with your woods or your technique around the greens, plump for the latter. After all, think of a player like Bernard Gallacher, who not only captained three Ryder Cup teams, but also competed in eight. This was a man who was fairly unimpressive off the tee, but more than made up for it with tenacity and confidence around the greens. There's no way that he would have achieved all he did in the game if his skills had been the other way round, where he had been great off the tee, but possessed an average short game.

Wedges

Once every self-respecting professional would carry four woods in his bag. Then John Daly decided, if it was all the same to everybody else, that he would prefer four wedges. People laughed at him. Daly, with one wood in his bag, then won the USPGA Championship without the benefit of a practice round. People laughed no more.

Conventional wisdom suggests that two wedges will get the job done. A pitching wedge will allow you to play not only the shots that the name suggests, but also little chips from around the green. With a

sand wedge you can obviously play bunker shots, and also 'flop' shots where you need to land the ball softly on the putting surface.

So why would you need any more? Isn't three or four enough for any player – amateur or professional? Barry Willet, for many years Mizuno's club maker on the European Tour, says it has everything to do with the design of modern courses. 'It is something that has happened in the last few years. Before, the pros would probably have had a standard wedge at 50 degrees and a sand-iron at 56.'

'Then they started getting into more bunkers around greens so now they like their sand-iron between 56 and 58 degrees (modern bunkers tend to be wider and longer and so the player requires the extra loft for more height to enable the ball to land softly). If their standard wedge is set at 50 that gives them quite a big gap, so they tend to carry a wedge in between set at 54 and, in Daly's case, a lobber wedge at 60.'

A third wedge is useful for the amateur who would rather hit a full shot as often as possible. Clearly, a 60 degree wedge enables you to hit a 60yd shot with a full swing, rather than a half-shot with a normal wedge, or a three-quarter one with a sand wedge. Jamie Spence makes this point: 'I get more use out of an extra sand wedge than I would out of a two iron because it gives me many more options. At a lot of new courses like East Sussex National, where the greens are fast and there is a lot of rough around them, you get a lot of different lies and you need three wedges.'

So there is the argument in favour. I tend to think that a newcomer to the sport would get more confused by, rather than benefit from, three wedges.

▼ **Modern bunkers tend to be wider and longer, so to combat this trend a sand wedge with extra loft is required.**

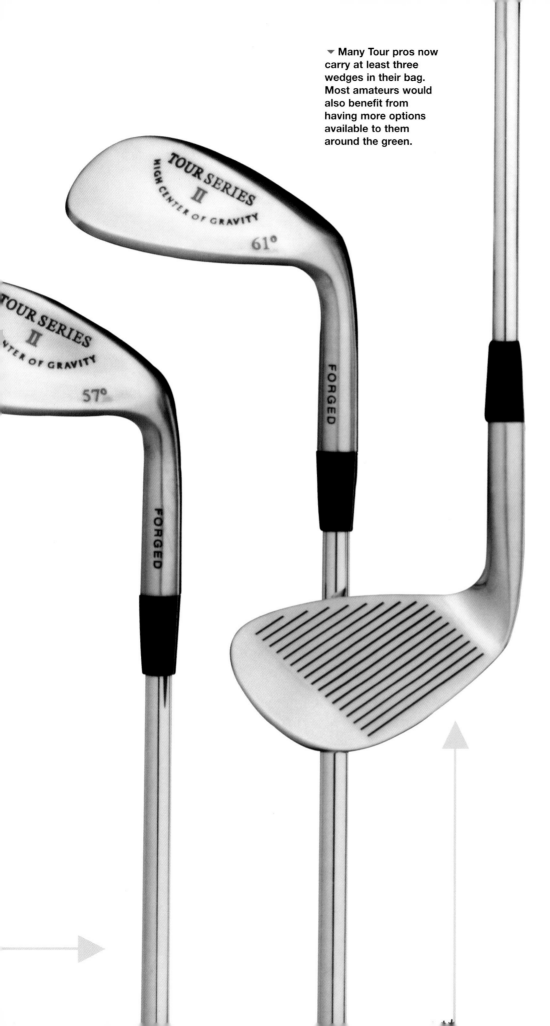

▼ Many Tour pros now carry at least three wedges in their bag. Most amateurs would also benefit from having more options available to them around the green.

Putting – the black art

▲ **American golfer Phil Mickelson is renowned for his silky-smooth putting stroke and his delicate touch on the greens.**

It is perhaps the greatest paradox in sport that something that anyone can play and enjoy without any tuition should also be the one thing that destroys careers because people have failed to master it.

No-one epitomized the impossible black art of putting more than Sam Snead, whom many consider the finest swinger of a golf club of all time, yet who was reduced to putting 'croquet style' because of his problems on the greens.

Bernhard Langer is the most famous sufferer in recent years. Three times he has been inflicted with the acute golfing condition known as the 'yips', and we deal in detail with this debilitating yet fascinating ailment later in this book. But isn't it truly amazing that men who can conquer the mysterious dynamics of the golf swing with seemingly effortless ease are left blabbering wrecks by the easiest stroke of all? Surely there is nothing too difficult in trying to propel a ball 1.68ins in diameter into a hole that is more than twice the size?

Ah, but this is the black art, remember. When an American company devised a putting machine and carried out tests in perfect and constant conditions, they were amazed to find that it could not hole every putt. The machine was in perfect working order; the human element had been taken away – it was now all down to simple geometry and physics. And still it missed from time to time.

The leading practitioners of the black art are blessed indeed, and their putters have become almost as famous as themselves. Ben Crenshaw's putter is known as 'Little Ben', and when it went missing for a time, the American was distraught. Since it was returned he has never let it out of his sight. If he goes on an aeroplane, he takes it on board with him. When checking in at a tournament his clubs are left in storage, but the putter goes back with him to the hotel room.

A person who putts well can often be quite a source of grievance to other golfers, particularly in matchplay competitions – it's as if they are using some sort of unfair method to win. Ben Hogan, a poor putter, once growled at Billy Casper, who wasn't: 'If you couldn't putt, you'd be selling hot-dogs outside the ropes.'

It isn't just the most intense players who suffer either. Mark James, as philosophical as they come, has been reduced to using a broomhandle putter.

It is plausible to conclude that good putters are born that way, blessed with a natural sense of feel, hand-to-eye co-ordination, and confidence. Yet even that isn't the whole tale. Good putters can easily lose their talent. Look at Tom Watson, from 1975 to 1985 one of the greatest putters that the game has seen, and one of the worst from 1985 to the present day.

The final proof that putting is indeed a black art comes on those occasions, which have happened to all of us, when we stand over a putt and just know that we are about to hole it. What mysterious force is at play here? What is happening to allow us to see the line as clear as day and know that the putt is going to drop? And why does it never last and why, three or four putts later, is everything about as clear as mud again?

It was at the 1967 Ryder Cup that one golf writer, who is best left nameless, was approached in the exhibition tent by an odd-looking little man with a goatee beard who was rattling on about a putter he had invented. He insisted that the writer have two and try them out. The writer did. He couldn't get on with them. He gave them away. Years later he was rather sorry he did this. Two of the first Ping putters off the production line – for that is what they were, and the man with the goatee beard was the inventor Karsten Solheim – would be worth rather a lot of money today.

◄◄ Bernhard Langer's long-running battle against the 'yips' saw him adopt a broomhandle putter.

Seven to nine irons

Technique

When using either a seven, eight, or nine iron, there is no great change in general technique from using the longer clubs mentioned in the previous chapter (The Long Game, see page 50). The shafts are shorter than with the long irons and so the knee bend should be a little more pronounced and the forearms more relaxed. The ball should also be positioned in your stance halfway between the middle of your feet and your left toe.

1 Because you are standing nearer to the ball, your posture when hitting a short iron, such as a nine iron, will be a little more angular than when hitting a longer iron. Other than that, there is no major difference in the set-up.

2 As with the pitching wedge, it is unlikely that you will need to swing the club back to the horizontal. If you retain the flex and resistance in your right knee, this is about as far back as you should go with a short iron.

3 Irons are designed to be struck with a slightly more descending blow than the driver and fairway woods which require a more shallow angle of attack. Don't be afraid to hit down and through the ball and always look to take a divot.

Because the shafts are shorter, you will be standing closer to the ball and with less freedom to turn the shoulders, your backswing will inevitably not be as long as it would be with your driver. This is a good thing as the key with these shots is control and accuracy. Clearly if your backswing is slightly shorter, then that offers more control, and more control means more accuracy.

Never try to force a short iron. You often hear of professionals hitting a 'hard' seven iron, but if you think a shot calls for everything you've got with an eight iron, then opt for smoothness and rhythm and hit a seven. It is impossible to over-stress that the key

with short irons is that distance doesn't get you any brownie points. Off the tee an extra 20yds might set up an easier second shot, but, with a short iron, it is getting the ball close to the pin that counts. You are much more likely to achieve that with a smooth eight rather than a hard seven. This is one area where adopting the ideas of the top pros can harm your own game. Because a player is standing that much closer to the ball and not as much can go wrong owing to the shorter shaft, it is usually not long before a player gains real confidence with these clubs. A few crisp short iron shots out of the middle of the club and everyone starts to get the golfing bug.

Quick tip

On shorter par threes, you will occasionally be hitting anything from a seven iron to a wedge; something to be avoided is to tee up the ball at the normal height. For these shots, many good players will dispense with a tee altogether on the grounds that they will get more feel without one. But if you feel more comfortable with a tee, make sure it is firmly stuck in the ground and the ball nestling just the merest smidgen off the turf.

▶▶ When you tee the ball up on a par three, make sure that the peg is pressed well into the ground so that only the tip of it is visible above the grass.

Seven to nine irons (2)

When to use and how far to hit

As we have already stated, the vast majority of full seven to nine iron shots will be used to fire to greens. However, these clubs are also good trouble-shooters. Occasionally you'll find yourself having to hit a nine iron over trees to relocate your fairway or a punched seven iron out of woodland back on to the mown stuff, but hopefully not too often.

The seven iron, however, can play a greater part in the decision-making process. If, for example, you are playing a par five that you can reach with a driver, three iron, and a wedge, but you don't like hitting a three iron and you are worried that it will leave you in trouble, you may consider hitting a driver and then two seven irons. The most important thing in golf is to get the job done and if it is a little unorthodox then so be it.

From the moment you consider your game good enough to step out regularly onto a golf course, you need to know how far you hit your short irons. Earlier in this book (see page 77), I suggested a simple tip to help you find out. The alternative is to learn the hard way: to find yourself with a 135yd shot over water; to say to yourself that it looks like a nine iron; and then strike it beautifully, watch it adoringly, expecting it to nestle next to the flag and see it instead go splash. Anyone who has been through this experience quickly learns how far he can hit each club.

▼ When a tree blocks your route to the green, you have to decide whether to go over it or under it. Unless you are confident of clearing the top of the branches, punch the ball underneath instead.

▶▶ If your route to the green is completely blocked by a tree, chip sideways where possible, or even take a penalty drop. Don't risk breaking your hands or the club by attempting a full shot.

Quick tip

When practising your shorter irons, make sure that you have a target at which to aim. These are the clubs, of course, that you will invariably be using to locate the greens and so you need to be deadly accurate. Try sticking an umbrella into the ground and aim to get within 30ft of it at least 75 per cent of the time.

◀◀ If your backswing is totally restricted by a tree, take your medicine and chip the ball out sideways and back onto the fairway.

Seven to nine irons (3)

Divot, heavy rough and flying lie

The short irons have adequate loft to deal with heavy rough, and the rougher it is, the shorter iron you will need. Clearly if you are up to your neck in it, you may have to consider taking an unplayable lie, but the general rule is that if you can see it, or any part of it, then a sand wedge will be able to get the ball out.

▶▶ A steep backswing is required to hit down through the ball and remove it from the long rough.

◀◀ When the ball is lying in heavy rough, don't get too greedy. Getting the ball back in play first time is your priority. Don't waste several shots for the sake of an extra 10yds carry.

▲ A grass stain on the sweet spot is the tell-tale sign that you have hit a flyer. Expect the ball to travel further than you anticipated.

◀◀ When blades of grass get trapped between the ball and the clubface at impact, it removes backspin from the shot causing the ball to fly further than normal. While amateurs will enjoy this, the pros dislike the lack of control.

What is most important when playing from heavy rough is to keep your eye on the ball. The temptation is to lift the head early in order to witness your miraculous recovery shot. However, there will be no miraculous recovery shot if you do.

Playing from heavy rough is one instance when you can swing the club harder than normal, but not if extra power comes at the expense of rhythm. You still have to have complete control of the clubhead as there is always the danger that the ball will not budge, or not budge enough for you to relocate it onto the fairway.

A flying lie is a ball situated in the first cut of rough, with a cushion of grass under the ball. That grass comes between the clubface and the ball and ends any chance a player has of imparting spin, so the ball ends up flying much further than normal. You'll soon be able to deduce whether you have a flying lie or not. The ball feels extremely sweet off the clubface but clearly, if it is flying 20yds more or so, the final result might not be so sweet. But once you have detected a flying lie, you can make allowances and take a club less than normal if you are playing to the green.

Pitching

General technique

The short game is primarily about confidence, but if your technique is incorrect then confidence will always elude you. There are four shots you need to master around the greens and if you can achieve a degree of solidity with each of them, then you are well on your way to lowering your handicap dramatically. The four are: the pitch, the chip, the bunker shot, the putt. The pitch covers various shots from 100yds from the flag, but generally what we are

1 When pitching into the green, the emphasis is on control and accuracy not power, so open your stance a little and stand slightly closer to the ball than for a full shot.

2 Depending on the length of the shot, you will need to make a slightly shorter swing than normal simply because you're not looking to hit the ball as far.

3 Don't fall into the trap of trying to scoop the ball into the air with your hands. Rotate your body through the ball and release the clubface to the target.

talking about here is the lobbed shot landing the ball softly on the green. The object is to get height on the ball and impart backspin. The pleasing thing from your point of view is that, equipped with the sand wedge you already have just the club for the task.

The basic pitch shot requires a half swing: you take the club back to the horizontal and then through to the same position. Place the ball in the centre of your stance with your weight on the left side. Your stance should be slightly open, with your shoulders pointing to the left of the target as you view it. Your hands should be ahead of the ball. It is here, before even starting the shot, that most beginners fall down. They want to put most of their weight on the right side and their hands behind the ball in order to scoop the ball into the air. The results are always disastrous – as I said, the sand wedge is equipped to do all the work.

Having got the right address position, you're more than halfway to completing your task. Simply swing the club normally to the horizontal and then back through the ball. Don't try to help it into the air, and don't quit on the shot – swing normally and smoothly. A modicum of practice and this becomes one of the easiest, but one of the most vital, shots in any golfer's repertoire. In every round there will be at least one or two occasions when a pitch shot is called for. Approach it with dread and you'll need three or four or even more shots to complete the hole; but approach it with confidence, and you will start to fancy your chances of getting down in two. Once you reach that happy state of affairs, you will really start to enjoy your golf.

◀◀ The short-range pitch shot is all about total control. Take a fairly narrow stance and set your hands ahead of the ball.

Quick tip

This is one shot when your head must remain still until after you have made contact with the ball. Nick Faldo has adopted the practice of not taking his eye off where the ball lay until his club has reached the horizontal on the follow-through. If you are prone to looking up before you have made contact with the ball this is one tip for you to try.

Full pitch

Playing 80yds from the green leaves you plenty of options: a canny low shot with a nine iron; a half shot with a pitching wedge; or a full blown pitch with a sand wedge. If there is water in front of the green or a hazard, then the last is your best option – unless you're playing into a strong breeze, in which case go with the wedge and hit a three-quarters shot.

There is no need to adopt any strange techniques with a full pitch shot. Just swing as you would with the wedge. Again, because the shaft is the shortest

1 The secret to playing pitch shots of any length is maintaining a smooth rhythm throughout the swing. Many golfers rush things when they have to abbreviate their backswing. Avoid this at all costs.

2 It can be tempting to look up too early to see where the ball has finished – particularly if you're not a confident pitcher. But you'll like what you see far more if you stay down through the shot and only take a peek once you've struck the ball.

3 Some top players will hold the clubface open through impact in an attempt to impart more backspin on the ball. You can try this, but you will probably be more consistent if you release the club normally.

in your bag, you will not be able to complete the backswing. This is not a problem.

Adopt your normal stance for a short iron shot. Once more, the key elements are rhythm and control. Make sure you accelerate through the ball and aim for a crisp, sure contact. The sand wedge is one club you should not force under any circumstances, but to a pin cut tight behind a bunker or to a small green, it is a most useful weapon.

4 You probably won't generate enough swing speed through the ball to make it into a full finish, so there's nothing wrong with a slightly abbreviated follow-through to match the length of your backswing.

Pitching over a bunker

Pitching over a bunker is ten per cent technique and ninety per cent confidence. There are two pitfalls that always trap the unwary beginner:

1. They're so worried about the shot that they 'quit' on it, decelerating into the hitting area. Wrists go rigid and the swing stutters. The result is that they hit behind the ball and it trickles into the very bunker they're trying to avoid, or, even more humiliatingly, stops short – therefore they've got the same shot to play over again.

1 When you need to get the ball up in the air quickly, open your stance at address and play the ball towards your front foot. The technique you will use is very similar to that employed from a bunker.

2 To create extra height on the shot, pick the club up fairly steeply with your hands and wrists as soon as you can in your backswing.

2. They're so worried about the shot that they're looking to see where it has finished, even before they've completed the backswing. The result is that they 'thin it' and the ball flies past the target at great speed, invariably leaving the player in a similar predicament over the other side of the green.

Clearly the key that links both these pitching shots is the fear of botching it up. The bunker is no longer just a hazard but a snarling menace, with an insatiable desire for your golf ball. Another common failing is the worry that the club does not possess enough loft to get the ball over the sand, so the player tries to scoop it over. Nothing could more certainly lead to failure.

First things first: make sure your technique is correct. The ball should be set in the middle of your stance; the weight should slightly favour the left-hand side. The most important aspects now are control and rhythm. The best way to ensure the former is with a backswing restricted to half your normal length – any more than that and you're asking for trouble. The follow-through will almost certainly be about the same length if you have mastered the rhythm. Swing normally. Think smooth and keep your legs still. Let the club do the work – it will have more than enough loft to get the ball over the bunker.

Once you have mastered these techniques, the next step is to conquer your mind. If you are sure in your technique then the bunker goes back to its role of being just another hazard. Now the shot is all about confidence and feel. Practise it enough and both come automatically. In time you'll be able to play this shot not just with a sand wedge, but also with a wedge and a nine iron as well, depending on the height of the bunker.

Being an accomplished exponent of this pitching shot is guaranteed to save you strokes every round. It also stops you falling victim to one of the most destructive elements in the sport. There's nothing worse than covering a 400yd hole in two and then marking down a six because you've needed two pitch shots. There's no hidden mystery as to why you felt you played well and yet you struggled to break three figures. If you can't pitch, you can't score. It's as simple as that.

3 To maximize the loft on the clubface and to generate height on the ball, keep the grooves on the clubhead facing the sky through impact and well into your follow-through.

Think half and half: half a backswing and half a follow-though. The swing should involve a slight acceleration through the ball, but not so much that it disturbs your rhythm. That is all important. If you're ever at a professional tournament, just wander over to the practice ground and watch the professionals working on this shot. One thing will be quickly apparent: their half-swings all possess the same tempo and all are as smooth as silk.

Bermuda rough

For those of us brought up on a staple diet of the chip and run shot, playing in America is often a humiliating experience. There you will find a great many courses have been seeded with Bermuda grass around the greens. Bermuda grass is tough and feisty and when your ball lands in a two-inch crop, it doesn't sit up as in Britain but plunges downwards. This is why you find many Americans will chip with a wedge or even a sand wedge.

Bermuda greens are lightning fast and so the object is to play a shot that has all the properties of a chip which will roll upon landing, but to play it like a pitch so that it just flops gently onto the green without rolling.

If you are playing a course with Bermuda grass for the first time, you will be happy if you can keep any chip on the green. When European golfers first try their hand on the US Tour, they always struggle and this is invariably because they are learning to cope

▼ **Playing out of Bermuda rough can be a humbling experience because it's almost impossible to judge exactly how the ball come out of the thick grass.**

1 To stand any chance of removing the ball from Bermuda-style rough, set up with your weight favouring your front foot and with your hands ahead of the ball. Ideally you want to hit down sharply on the ball so that it pops up into the air.

with the peculiarities of this pitch-cum-chip shot.

More and more courses are now using grasses that cause the ball to sit down in the rough around the greens. I think this Americanization of British courses is a great shame, but if you play at such a course or travel abroad a fair deal, then it's something with which you need to come to terms.

Adopt your normal pitching stance, keeping the hands well ahead of the ball. The object is to hit the ball with a downwards blow so that it pops out of the rough. Keep the rhythm smooth and keep accelerating through the ball – any deceleration and the Bermuda will wrap itself around the clubface and the ball will move about two inches. It's a shot that requires a fair bit of patience and practice. If the only time you encounter it is on your golfing holiday every other year – don't worry about it and don't let it spoil your round!

2 Bermuda grass is deceptively and notoriously thick and tangly. Don't expect to be able to make much of a follow-through if you have played the shot correctly.

Divot

With luck you will never have to face playing a pitch shot from a divot. But sometimes you will play a course where there is a hole that leaves a player a 40yd pitch shot over water and here you might find a gathering of divots and your ball may well finish in one of them.

Yes, by all means, take a couple of seconds to curse your luck, but this is really another shot which looks worse than it is. Once more, adopt your normal stance for a pitch shot: the ball in the middle of your feet; your weight predominantly on your left side; your shoulders and feet slightly open to the target.

Your object here is for the club to meet the back of the ball just before taking a smidgen of turf, and the best way for you to do this is with a controlled half backswing, leading to a smooth acceleration through the ball. Once you've successfully completed this shot you will be surprised how much of the fear has evaporated the next time.

▲ When your ball falls into a divot it can often look worse than it actually is. Remember to think calmly and logically work through the movements involved to create a successful pitch.

◀◀ It is a rule of etiquette associated with the game that every player should replace their divots. However, this isn't always the case, and you may need help to achieve the shot well.

Bare lie

A pitch shot from a bare lie is much more common. Even on the best links courses, the ground around the bunkers near the greens can get very parched. Many amateurs dread playing a pitch shot over a bunker from a bare lie.

The professionals would much rather face such a scenario than a cushioned lie because it enables them to impart spin on the ball. Once again this is a shot where basic technique will help you overcome any fears – the normal pitch shot rules apply.

Quick tip

If there are two common faults among the poor pitchers of this world, it is that they have their weight on the right-hand side in a misguided attempt to scoop the ball into the air, their backswing is too long and they therefore decelerate through the ball. Concentrate on these two things and the days of poor pitching will soon belong to your previous life.

1 From a bare or hard-pan lie, it's imperative that you set up with your hands ahead of the ball at address to ensure a crisp strike. The last thing you want is for the clubhead to bounce off the ground into the back of the ball.

2 Through impact make sure that your hands return to exactly the same position that they occupied at address – a couple of inches ahead of the ball.

The shank

There are two words that should be avoided in golfing company and this is one of them. The other is the 'yips', a degenerative putting disease that has finished the careers of many great golfers. But the shank is the shot that all average players fear the most because it is the most destructive shot in the game to affect them. It occurs when the face of the blade is open at impact and the club has been swung on an incorrect path. The ball comes off the hosel instead of the club face and squirts away at right angles to the target.

The worst thing about the shank is how quickly it can become a habit. Once it has happened, it can rapidly infect the mind and if things reach that stage, then standing over a pitch shot becomes very fearful for the demoralized player.

1 A shank occurs when the ball is struck by the hosel of the club (the point where the clubhead meets the shaft) instead of the clubface.

2 The reason why so many golfers fear the shot is because it shoots off sharply to the right, normally into the rough, trees or out of bounds.

The first corrective stage is in the set-up: make sure the ball is in the middle of your stance; that your weight is on your left side; the shoulders and feet are slightly open to the target; and the ball is positioned in the middle of your club face when you set the club down and not opposite the hosel. Now the backswing: take the club back to the horizontal, resisting any temptation to roll the wrists early; feel that you are in control on the downswing, that you have retained your rhythm, and that you are not decelerating as you come towards the ball. The best way for you to control the impact is with a half-backswing, leading to a smooth acceleration through the ball. Once you've successfully completed this shot, you'll be surprised how much of the fear has evaporated the next time.

Quick tip

Correcting the odd shank is not a difficult thing to do and you may find that you will go for years before you suffer another. But if it is commonplace in your game, then your muscles have been trained to work in a certain, incorrect way and you've got problems. Explaining the way out of this problem in a book is one thing, but you may want to seek professional advice to teach yourself where the club should be and so retrain your muscles.

1 To reduce your chances of hitting a shank, make sure that your posture is good and that the ball is correctly positioned towards the centre of your stance. Check your grip pressure, too, making sure that it's not too tight as this will prevent you from releasing the club correctly.

2 Focus on swinging the club along the target line and avoid any sudden changes of swing path or tempo. Always commit to the shot since easing up and decelerating the clubhead actually increases your chances of shanking.

The flop shot

No, this isn't the description given to a make or break shot that you mess up. The flop shot is a highly-skilled pitch, where the player imparts so much backspin on the ball that it ascends almost vertically before stopping abruptly.

For all his reputation as a long-hitter, John Daly is also one of the masters of this shot. I once saw him play the second hole in the Open at Muirfield and, having almost driven the green at this shortish par four, he had left himself the following shot: a pitch

1 The flop shot from the rough is similar to the splash shot from the sand. Open your stance and the clubface at address and play the ball well forward to maximize the amount of height you generate.

2 As with the bunker shot you must make almost a full backswing when hitting a flop shot, since because of the excessive amount of loft you're looking to achieve, it can be difficult to generate forward momentum.

3 Commit to swinging along the line of your feet – not along the target line – and trust the loft on your sand wedge or lob wedge to do all the work for you. Always remember to accelerate the clubhead through the grass otherwise you'll struggle to move the ball very far.

from a bare lie over a bunker, with the pin cut 10ft from the sand.

I thought he would have to play for the safe half of the green and settle for a four. I couldn't see any other option. Daly could – he took out his 60 degree

4

Where possible, keep your backswing and follow-through the same length for maximum control, but if the rough is really thick you may struggle to swing through to a full finish.

wedge, almost completed a full backswing and to a stunned audience hit the ball very hard. It was propelled vertically, must have risen 30ft in the air, landing just over the bunker before finishing next to the hole.

Phil Mickelson, another American brought up on these lofted wedges, once completed the following shot in a college event: trying to play short of a ditch in front of the green, he miscalculated to the extent that the ball rolled down towards the ditch, but came to rest on the downslope. He couldn't see how he could get the ball up quickly enough from this downward lie to clear the ditch, so he turned the other way. The spectators thought he was just chipping the ball back on to the fairway from whence he came; but Mickelson thrashed at the ball with all his might and it stayed on the clubface so long that it went back over his head, over the ditch, and on to the front of the green.

How to play that shot only Mickelson knows, just as only Daly knows how he got that tap-in birdie at Muirfield, but playing a variation of the flop shot is within the grasp of most players.

Adopt your normal pitching stance with the blade slightly open, (you need a slightly fuller swing than usual) and accelerate through the ball – it is the clubhead speed that imparts the backspin and gets the ball up quickly.

Quick tip

For heaven's sake don't try this shot for the first time when playing on the golf course. For players like Mickelson and Daly, it took years of practice and, if you don't pull it off, you could find that your acceleration through the ball has propelled it into somebody's back garden. The flop shot is a useful weapon to have, but there are plenty of others that need to be given higher priority.

Practice

1 Learn to visualize the shot. Before you actually try to play the pitch shot you've left yourself, it is important to make a mental note of what you are trying to achieve, something you can learn on the practice ground. Try playing to a practice green and visualize each time the shot you're trying to execute. Picture where the ball is going to land on the green and aim for that spot.

2 Get into the same mental routine whenever you're confronted with a pitch shot. Commit the following check list to memory: a) Have I visualized the shot I want to play? b) Is the ball in the middle of my stance, with my feet no more than 15ins apart? c) Is most of my weight on my left hand side, thus promoting a crisp contact with the ball? d) Are my shoulders open and therefore pointing to the left of the target? Finally: half a backswing and half a follow-through.

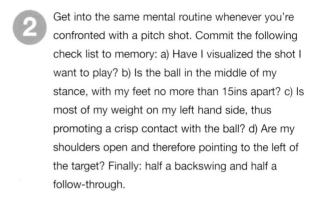

3 If you've lost confidence completely with your pitching, then separate each of the fundamentals and practice them in turn. First practise the half swing without a ball at your feet. Let your muscles feel what you're actually asking of them. Now practise with your weight on your left hand side and feel the bottom of the club just touching the ground at what would be the point of impact. Now try it with a ball in front of you. Keep the same smooth rhythm and build up your confidence.

4 The mistake that many people make when they are practising pitch shots is to do so from a perfect lie each time and then they're puzzled as to why they make a mess of a shot from a difficult lie when they are out on the course. Try practising a few pitch shots from the rough, and also from bare lies. Simulate what happens on the course. Instead of thinking about perfect lies, turn the equation round. If you can master pitch shots from bare lies and the rough then when you get a perfect one it will be no problem at all.

Quick tip

The practice ground isn't just for working on your technique. Use your time at the range to develop a consistent pre-shot routine that you will be able to rely on under pressure.

Chipping

8

1 Consistency of strike is the key to good chipping. To increase your chances of a crisp strike, ease your weight onto your front foot and play the ball just back of centre in your stance. Last but not least, make sure that your hands are ahead of the ball.

2 The chip shot is played predominantly with the arms with very little wrist action. While it's perfectly acceptable for the wrists to 'give' a little in response to the weight and momentum of the clubhead, you shouldn't consciously involve them at any stage.

3 Even in the follow-through there is no sign whatsoever of any wrist action. The hands have remained passive throughout and the whole action has been controlled by the arms and shoulders. It is usually advisable to keep your swing as compact as possible.

General technique

Chipping and pitching are often mixed up by complete beginners, but after you have read the previous chapter, the difference should be obvious. The chip is played with a straighter-faced club and is designed for the ball to clear a cut of rough and then roll to the pin. Professionals have chipping down to such a fine art that even when playing to an uneven green with many borrows to negotiate, they always expect to get down in two shots. With a little practice you too should be able to get down in two on many occasions. The chip is one shot in which you need to have a lot of faith in yourself. It's a bread-and-shot and will serve you well on far more occasions than the pitch, unless you're playing a course with lots of bunkers and small greens.

It is also a very easy shot to play as it can be played with any club from a seven iron through to a wedge, so select one from your bag. Now, adopt your normal stance, but stand a little closer to the ball and hold the club lightly towards the bottom of the grip. Control is everything with the chip shot and so gripping a little firmer down the shaft will help in this respect.

The ball should be in the middle of your stance and your weight predominantly on your left hand side. Keep your hands ahead of the ball and your knees slightly bent. From this position you will strike the ball on a downward arc which will promote spin and negate any chance of hitting the ground first. Clearly the length of the chip shot will dictate how far you should go on your backswing but you shouldn't have to go back more than 3ft, even for the longest chip. Keep it smooth and rhythmical. No need to worry about unhinging your wrists: the chip is an extension of the putting stroke. Finally, keep your eye on the ball. So many chips are ruined because the player is looking to see how he has done before the stroke has been completed and the result is always a destructive thinned shot, which invariably scuttles through the green and leaves, at best, exactly the same chip shot coming back.

Quick tip

Whenever my chipping goes off and I'm striking the ball improperly, I concentrate on keeping my legs as still as possible. There should be no leg movement when you're playing a chip shot. If the legs are still, the arms can move freely back and forth through the ball, thus ensuring the correct contact.

Pitching versus chipping

The headline is perhaps a little misleading, as it suggests that there is a contest between the two and that when you miss a green, you are engaged in a battle of wills between whether to pitch the ball back on to the putting surface or to chip it.

In fact it is not quite like that. If the option to chip the ball is available, then chip it – it's as simple as that. The greater the loft when playing a shot around the green then the greater the chance of error. Let's take a few examples:

1 A fairly steep, closely-mown bank lies between you and the plateau green, with just 10ft of the putting surface to work with before the flag. Pitch or chip? Chip it up the bank with a six or seven iron, or even a putter if you feel more comfortable with it. The odds on pitching it and getting it to stop close to the pin are very small and if you miscalculate on the short side, the ball is going to come back and finish at your feet.

2 You're in heavy rough just off the green with the pin 20yds away. You're pretty sure that if you took a seven iron, the clubface would become entangled

and you would lose control of the shot. Pitch or chip? Chip the ball with a wedge. Make sure you keep your hands ahead of the ball so you're 'chopping' down on it. The grass that will inevitably get between the head of the club and the ball means that it will still roll as if you had played it with a seven iron.

1 If a hazard, such as a bunker, blocks your way to the hole, a pitch shot is the correct choice because a chip shot won't have enough height to clear the sand.

3 A bunker lies between you and the pin, but the face is shallow, so there's no great need for height to get the ball over it. Pitch or chip? Depends on whether there is plenty of green with which to work. If there is, then a chip is your best bet. If not, then pitch it as the extra height will enable you to stop the ball quickly.

4 You've missed the first green by five yards, so now you've got 15yds to go to the flag with 15ft of rough to negotiate. Pitch or chip? Chip it. Aim to land the ball just on the fringe of the green and let it roll to the pin. It's basically a case of following the golden rule: only pitch when you have to.

2 The added benefit of extra loft is that the ball will land softly once it hits the green. With a chip shot the ball will tend to run much more on landing.

1 With nothing between your ball and the flag, the chip shot is the more sensible option and you should keep the ball as low to the ground as possible to reduce the risk.

2 As with any shot, it's important to stay down through the ball and resist the temptation to have a sneaky look at how well you have judged the shot.

Buried lie

Playing a pitch shot from a buried lie or deep rough is as much a test of your course management skills as technique. Clearly you are going to lose much of your control over the shot, so what you need to assess is the extent of the trouble that lies between you and the pin and beyond. Is there a bunker to negotiate? A water hazard lurking on the other side of the green?

A bogey from the position in which you have left yourself would not be a disaster, but you do not want to end up with a double bogey or worse. If the lie is bad and there is a water hazard lying in wait, play away from it, even if it means playing for a part of the green where the flag is not in residence. One of the things to remember about this shot is not to panic and go thrashing at the ball thinking it is the only way that it will come out. Unless the lie is truly dire, the basic pitch shot will serve you well enough.

Concentrate on your 'half to half' swing and aim to make as clean a contact as you can. Remember to take into account that there will be little spin on the ball, so once it hits the ground it will behave more like a chip shot and roll a considerable distance.

▶▶ **This shot can often seem daunting but if you keep the body still and the wieght equally distributed your success rate will be much higher.**

▶▶ **Always think through your options before choosing your shot. It may be that a clean contact cannot be achieved, so look to play a percentage club in order to find your way back on course, rather than thrashing for the green and failing to get clear of the rough.**

Quick fact

There's no denying that the one thing you really need when playing a pitch shot from a buried lie is a bit of luck. Thus did Mark Calcavecchia survive an anxious moment in the 1989 Open at Royal Troon. At the 12th hole he not only had a poor lie, but also a bunker to negotiate. He committed the cardinal sin. His rhythm was jerky and his head was up too quickly. The result was he thinned the shot and was headed for all sorts of trouble on the other side of the green – until the pin got in the way. Calcavecchia's ball finished in the hole for the unlikeliest of birdies and he went on to win the event in a four-hole play-off.

Behind a bunker

If a bunker lies between a player and the pin, many people reach automatically for the sand wedge to pitch the ball back on to the green. Yet this shouldn't have to be the case. How steep is the face of the bunker? How much green do you have to work with to the flag? Instead of trying to flop the ball back on to the green and therefore risk flopping it into the sand, a chip with a nine iron or even a pitching wedge would be a more sensible alternative if the bunker is shallow.

Also, look to see if there is a way you can negotiate around the sand. In the 1976 Open at Birkdale, Severiano Ballesteros announced his arrival to the golfing world with just such a shot. At the 18th hole in the final round, his second shot had put him to the left of the green seemingly with a couple of bunkers to go over and little green with which to work. Yet the Spaniard confirmed his genius by playing a little chip instead through the small channel between the bunkers to 3ft. It looked a miraculous shot, but in fact the option he chose was a far easier one than trying to pitch it close.

Fringe of the green

Similarly, when on the fringe of the green, most players reach automatically for the putter. In many cases, if the ground in front of them looks smooth, this is the correct option. But many will use it even if the ground is rough and then become annoyed when the ball 'takes off' as soon as they hit it, either bouncing away or pulling up miles short. Consider using a five or six iron and chipping the ball using your putting stroke. You don't have to alter anything, but the difference is that the ball will carry over the first few feet of rough ground before rolling toward its final resting place beside the pin.

▸▸ **Experimenting around the greens can pay huge dividends, as was the case when Fred Couples holed a shot from off the green using the toe of his putter to strike the ball.**

When chipping around the green with a five or six iron, consider using not just your putting stroke but a putting grip as well. To do this, rest the index finger of your left hand over the middle fingers of your right hand. This may feel strange at first, but it is a grip that promotes feel, and feel is what this shot is all about.

Which club?

This is a source of considerable debate within the game: should I chip with a seven iron, nine iron, wedge, sand wedge, or putter? My answer would be to chip with them all (not at the same time, however) and throw in an eight iron for good measure as well.

But not at first. If you are a raw beginner, chip with a seven iron for the first few months. Practise with it in the back garden and learn its trajectory and how hard you need to hit the ball to make it travel a certain distance. Then you can start to experiment.

Many professionals, though, return to chipping with just one club (usually a wedge). They find a certain loss of feel if they swap and change between clubs. Most, though, operate by a hard and fast rule that has stuck for several generations: its basic principle is to chip with the club you need to clear the uneven ground before the putting green and allow the ball to roll out to the flag. So, if you're 10ft from the putting surface and the pin is cut 25ft on the green you will need the club which you feel will propel the ball 25ft after landing (probably something like an eight iron). Watch how many professionals abide by this golden rule. Ultimately, however, chip with whichever club you feel most comfortable, as it is absolutely vital to stand over the shot and have total confidence that you are going to hit it close to the pin. If that means chipping with a driver, then so be it, which brings us nicely onto the next topic.

◀◀ **The important point here is to find the club that you are most comfortable with. Start with a seven iron, and then when you are happy with that, begin to experiment until you find a suitable club.**

▶▶ **Although his long game has deteriorated in recent years, Spain's Seve Ballesteros is still a magician around the greens and is a supreme chipper and putter.**

When considering what club to use from beyond the fringe of the green, don't forget to include the putter in your options, particularly if you have to get the ball up a steep bank off a tight lie. In circumstances such as this, the putter is often a safe bet: you might not get the ball as close to the pin as you would like, but equally it is unlikely that you will totally mess up.

Alternatives

Fred Couples caused quite a stir at the Masters a couple of years ago with his solution to a ball that was nesting in a little patch of rough just off the green. Couples chose to use his Ping putter, which was hardly radical although the lie didn't look the sort from which you could use such a club. But when Couples tried a couple of practice swings, it became clear he was going to strike the ball not in the conventional manner but with the toe of the putter.

This caused great excitement among the watching faithful. It caused great excitement all around the world when Couples played the shot to perfection. The toe of the putter eased itself under the ball, which landed on the green very, very gently before trickling down to the flag and into the hole.

A number of players have come up with different answers to different dilemmas, clearly adopting the maxim 'if needs must'. Many now use a driver or three wood to play a chip shot where the ball has come to rest against a little tuft of grass beside the green. They play the shot as if it was a putt but the vital difference is that the greater weight of the driver head means it does not get tangled up in the rough.

Many amateurs carry a special chipping iron in their bags, which generally have the same loft as a seven iron but are specifically designed solely for chipping, not for full shots as well.

Many senior players so love hitting their seven woods that they will often chip with the same club. Indeed, golfers have always invented different purposes for clubs than that originally intended. The chip is, in essence, such a simple shot that it was perhaps inevitable that it should attract more than its fair share of experimentation.

▶▶ **Ernie Els manages to get loft on the ball, despite an awkward stance and lie.**

◀◀ **In some situations, the humble putter can be the perfect club for a chip shot.**

In the sudden death play-off for the 1987 Masters, Larry Mize left himself the most difficult of shots after his approach to the 11th green had missed on the left. He had 140ft to go with all sorts of humps and hollows to negotiate and, while conventional wisdom suggested he should pitch the ball most of that distance with a wedge and let the ball run out to the hole, Mize followed his own counsel. He used a seven iron and rolled the ball this way and that, over all the uneven ground, before finally the ball came to rest in the hole for victory. Mize, the local boy, jumped for joy. How good a shot was it? Well, six months on, Mize was invited to try it again. He tried it 100 times. He never came close once.

Practice

1 As long as your back garden doesn't resemble a wild Borneo jungle, you can easily practise your chipping there. Just ten to 15 minutes every other day will promote a correct strike of the ball and teach you all you need to know about trajectory and distance. Stick an umbrella in the ground some 20yds away so you've got something to aim at.

2 Hopefully the golf club that you use will have a practice putting green that allows you to chip onto it as well. Here you can experiment with different clubs to see which you need for the ball to travel a certain distance once it has landed on the edge of the green.

3 As with pitching, it is very helpful to get into a mental routine before playing a chip shot. The practice ground is where you can learn to commit the following to memory:
a) Is my weight predominantly on my left hand side?
b) Is the ball in the middle of my stance and am I holding the club towards the bottom of the grip?
c) Are my hands ahead of the ball?
d) Have I got a clear picture of what I am trying to achieve with this chip shot?

4 Watch the professionals. Either by viewing on television or attending a tournament in person, to watch the top players do their stuff may be a source of great pleasure, but it rarely has anything to do with the game that you play. But around the greens it does, and particularly chip shots. Just watch the way every professional plays this stroke. The weight distribution; the hands ahead of the ball; the smooth controlled rhythm. This is one area of the game where you can not only watch and admire, but realistically seek to emulate as well.

◀◀ Watching the professionals is a great place to start in learning how to improve your game. Observing someone like Sergio Garcia using a chip shot will give you no end of tips and pointers for your own game.

9 Bunkers

Bunkers come in all shapes and sizes, for example at the Oxfordshire in England, the par five fourth hole features a bunker that is 100yds long by 45yds wide. At the short par four 14th there is a pot bunker that is only wide enough to swing a club.

Different types of bunkers and sand

Bunkers have long been steeped in mystique and the best of them are the stuff of legend. At many of the old links courses they have names, and at the Old Course at St Andrews the vast majority of them do, the most famous of them being the Road Hole bunker, a vast deep pit that protects half of the green at the 17th, the Road Hole. Some people refer to it as the Sands of Nakajima, after the unfortunate Japanese Tommy Nakajima who fell from grace in the 1978 Open after needing four shots to extricate himself; perhaps younger golfers will start referring to it as the Sands of Duval after the American suffered a similarly tortuous fate during the final round of the 2000 Open.

At the 14th, Hell Bunker stands some 100yds short of the green. It dates back to 1882 when one golfer, after a terrible round, complained to the St Andrews professional, Old Tom Morris, that the only decent lie he had was at the bottom of the deep bunker at the 14th, where he used a wood to get out. Morris, who didn't have much of a sense of humour at the best of times, is said to have dispatched a work crew there and then with the words, 'Come hell or high water, dig it so deep that no player will ever use a wood from there again'.

The original intention was that finishing in a bunker would cost a player a shot, but after Gene Sarazen invented the sand wedge, golfers began to save par with great regularity. Today, it has reached the stage where a normal bunker shot strikes no fear at all in the top professional, who will expect nine times out of ten to get down in two. This in turn has led to modern courses featuring more severe bunkers and contrived sand traps and it seems the only man who has lost out is the humble amateur who wasn't so enamoured with the conventional ones let alone those of a more intricate variety.

Yet, given the correct technique and a modicum of confidence, no player should take more than three shots to complete a hole from a greenside bunker. With today's equipment, anything worse than a bogey from a decent lie in the sand is a poor score indeed.

◄◄ The famous church pews row of bunkers at Oakmont, Pennsylvania, troubled Arnold Palmer in the 1994 US Open.

▶▶ Bunkers were originally designed to punish golfers, but they no longer hold any fear for the top players.

Quick fact

One of the most famous bunker shots of recent times was made by Bob Tway in the 1986 USPGA Championship at Inverness, Ohio. Playing the last hole, the American was tied with Greg Norman, but found a trap with his second shot. A play-off seemed the most likely scenario, with Norman an obvious favourite to win if it was all settled in normal time. That plot didn't take into account Tway's powers from the sand. He played the perfect shot, the ball landing 12ft from the pin before finishing in the hole.

Technique

Like the pitch shot, playing from a bunker is 20 per cent technique and 80 per cent confidence. Show me a golfer who regularly has trouble from the sand and I'll show you someone who hasn't mastered the basic fundamentals of playing the shot, yet they're so straightforward that an hour's practice from a bunker will do much to remove the fear of someone who is terrified of going into a sand trap.

The basic technique is this: make sure the ball is positioned in the centre of your stance; your feet and your shoulders should be open, that is pointing a little to the left of the target; make sure you have a firm stance in the bunker, and that the blade of the club is a little open as well.

What you are trying to do from now on is a half swing, as in the pitch shot. You're aiming to hit the sand some two inches behind the ball – you want to take a clean layer of sand, not dig for your country,

so don't thrash at it – just swing normally, but imagine that you're trying to swing an inch below the ball. One cardinal sin the amateur makes in a bunker is quitting on the shot; you must complete a full

To counteract the open clubface at address that is required to maximize the bounce on your sand wedge, open your stance so that your feet and body aim left of the target.

▼ **To make maximum use of the bounce angle on the sole of your sand wedge, open the clubface at address.**

rhythmical follow-through for successful results. If you have a longer bunker shot to play – say, about 30yds – then you want to hit the sand just one inch behind the ball using a three-quarter swing. The key to good bunker play is possessing the confidence to descend into the bunker knowing that at worst it will come out and at best it will finish close to the hole. Good technique will help you nurture that confidence.

2 Once you have aligned your body correctly, commit to swinging the club along the line of your feet and your body, not along the ball/target line. Make virtually a full swing to ensure that you create enough swing speed to remove the sand underneath the ball.

3 As you can see here, although the player has clearly swung the club along the line of his feet, the ball is flying straight towards the target – exactly where the clubface was aiming at address.

Quick tip

There's an easy way to learn how much sand to take: draw a line in the sand two inches behind the ball and two inches in front of it. Both these lines should be obliterated in order to play the shot properly. Of course you can only do this in practice: you're not allowed to touch the sand with your club or your finger under normal circumstances. One other thing which can't be stressed enough – make sure you complete the follow-through and swing smoothly through the ball. Conquer that fear!

Sloping lies

Uphill lie

An uphill lie presents a completely different set of circumstances. Here it shouldn't be any trouble at all getting the ball out of the sand. However, the problem is getting sufficient distance to get the ball to the flag, because the slope will act as a launch pad and send it straight into the air. Instead, position the ball a little further forward in your stance, but otherwise swing normally to propel the ball out of the sand trap. If the pin is a long way away then you should consider a three-quarters swing or using a pitching wedge to compensate.

1 From an upslope the ball will fly high and land softly. Your only problem will be generating enough distance on the shot, so you will need to make a full swing or use a pitching wedge instead.

2 Because the slope will throw the ball straight up into the air you will need to make a long backswing to create sufficient swing speed through the ball to carry it to the hole.

3 This is no situation for the faint-hearted. Commit yourself fully to the shot and don't be afraid to hit hard through impact as you stick the clubhead in the sand behind the ball.

Downhill lie

Finishing in the back of a bunker, contemplating a downhill lie, is an unhappy experience. If the green to which you are playing is small and there's trouble behind, then what you're left with is one of the hardest shots in the game. The most important thing to remember is not to let your fear show when you enter the bunker. Be in a positive frame of mind, believing that the ball is going to come out and stay on the green.

Occasionally, if the back wall of the bunker is steep, you will find yourself unable to make a proper backswing and in this case you will either have to take an 'unplayable' or come out sideways. However, such situations are rare and normally you can take a swipe at the ball. Position the ball a little further back in your stance to take account of the slope, but otherwise visualize, as normal, hitting the sand about two inches behind the ball. Here, more than ever, it is important to keep everything smooth and complete the follow-through.

4 The upslope will prevent you from swinging into a full finish, which makes it even more important for you to generate power through impact.

Depressed Lies

Fried Egg Lie

We've all experienced that sinking feeling: an iron shot heading for a bunker is bad enough, but when it gets there, it falls like a stone from the sky and ends up in a plugged lie (the fried egg as it is known).

To those players who are scared of bunkers anyway, this is a nightmare unfolding before their eyes. They flail at the ball with no real conception of how it is going to come out and of course it doesn't. Their confidence is so shattered that the next one probably doesn't come out either.

Using a wedge is always a good idea in these circumstances. It will cut through the sand more easily. Otherwise, the only other difference is to have a slightly fuller swing than you would normally use for a bunker shot of similar distance from a good lie. Remember too, that when the ball hits the green, it will have no spin on it and so roll forever.

Footprint Lie

Equally distressing is the ball that finishes in a footprint. Here, once more, a wedge may be your best option, depending upon how heavy the culprit was and how deep his footprint. If the ball is a fair way down, then use a wedge. Once more a positive attitude will work wonders here – you have the equipment to extricate the ball from such a situation, so don't enter the bunker thinking you have to swing yourself off your feet to get it out. You don't.

▸▸ When the ball is buried in the sand, think about using your pitching wedge to play the shot as it has a sharper leading edge.

▸▸ There's no need to open your stance when hitting a shot from a buried lie in the sand. Keep your stance square and swing along the line of your feet.

Quick fact

In some countries, and particularly in America, you will see huge bunkers known as waste bunkers on the sides of some fairways. These are the only bunkers where you are allowed to ground your club prior to beginning your stroke. You will know whether you are in a waste bunker by looking at the local rules on the back of the scorecard, which will identify them as such.

Wet sand

After long spells of rain, the sand in a bunker will obviously be wet and hard and exhibit different properties than when under normal circumstances. When you step into the bunker and go to take your stance, you will be able to gauge how hard the sand is and, if it has compacted, then a wedge will probably be the most suitable club. The reason is that the flange at the bottom of the sand wedge has been designed for use under circumstances that will prevail at least 90 per cent of the time.

However, if the sand has compacted, then the flange will bounce off it and you will hit the ball without being able to get underneath it. The result will be a thinned shot into the face of the bunker – either that or a thinned shot that clears the face of the bunker and finishes in a hedge or someone's back garden. By contrast, the thinner leading edge of the wedge will allow you to cut through the compacted sand and play a bunker shot in the orthodox way. The only difference is that the wedge hasn't as much loft and so the ball will come out on a flatter trajectory and will roll further.

◄◄ Although you should play most bunker shots with your sand wedge, when the sand is wet and compacted, your pitching wedge, which has less bounce on the sole, is a better option.

▶▶ From a good lie in a bunker the top professionals are often looking to hole the shot, not just get the ball close. Compare that with your own attitude in the sand!

Shallow-faced bunker

Many players automatically reach for a sand wedge when their ball lands in a bunker, even if the trap has little or no lip to it. Their reasoning is: 'I am in sand therefore logically it must call for me to use a sand wedge'. And maybe it does, but think a little. If the ball is lying well in sand that is not of the fluffy kind that will stop the ball rolling, why not use a putter?

After all, what is to stop you? If the lip is low enough it will not stop the ball coming out and if the sand is firm, then the ball will roll. One thing to remember, of course, is that you will not be able to ground your putter behind the ball, just as you cannot ground your sand wedge in a bunker prior to impact.

Quick tip

If using a putter out of the sand, remember that you will need to hit the ball considerably harder than normal. Obviously don't go to extremes and thrash at it as you would a driver, but even if the sand is hard, it will slow the ball. So imagine that you are putting under the same resistance as if you were putting on your back lawn – always presuming, of course, that your back lawn is neither a bowling green nor untamed!

Putting

◀◀ Putters are very
personal pieces of
equipment. If you are
confident with how
your club looks and
feels it will reflect in a
more positive stroke.

Passing on advice for choosing a putter is almost like offering tips on selecting your ideal partner or what car to drive. I guess what I'm trying to say is that much of it comes down to personal opinion in the end.

Choosing a putter

As a result, when you enter your local golf emporium, you will be terribly spoilt for choice. Putters with exotic names – Nick Price won the 1994 USPGA Championship using one called 'The Fat Lady' (I bet it was a fat man who came up with the name). You'll see putters with short heads, putters with long heads, putters with straight heads, putters with triangular-shaped heads, putters with bulbous heads, putters with heads that have no frills at all.

Putters with broomhandle shafts, putters with thick grips, putters with . . . well I'm sure you've got the message by now.

Putting is such a psychological game that looks do matter. You need to like what you see. When you pick it up, it must feel the correct weight to you. Now take your stance behind the ball – does it sit nicely and enable you to line up to your target without having to make any adjustments?

Most important of all, when you strike a couple of putts is the ball coming naturally out of the sweetspot? Thinking cheaply can be a very expensive business when it comes to buying a putter.

You need one where you can find the sweetspot easily and when you strike it properly the ball rolls freely and fully, otherwise you'll be discarding it quickly and having to buy another one. If you're fairly new to the game, forget all thoughts of anything too fancy. Don't think about broom handle putters for instance, or putters with thick grips.

When Jack Nicklaus won the 1986 Masters, he did so with a putter that had an unusually large head, easily twice the normal size. MacGregor, the company to whom Nicklaus was signed at the time, soon had a version on the market, and it sold in the hundreds and thousands. But I bet hardly anyone is using one now, ten years on – Nicklaus certainly isn't, so beware of anything flash, any gimmicks.

Make sure as well that your putter is the right length for you. When you take your stance and hold the club your body should fall naturally into the address position. If you are scrunched over the ball, then the shaft is too short for you. If you stand bolt upright, then it is clearly too long.

On the question of weight, this is something that is of personal preference, but ideally you want to steer clear of anything too lightweight because your timing will be affected and consequently the quality of strike will be impaired.

Finally, don't expect to find your ideal putting partner in the first place you look. Indeed you may find yourself going through several relationships before you find the one for you. It may be the grandest thing in the shop or it may be as ugly as sin, but what is vital is that you get along just fine. And if that is the case care for it, cherish it through the good times – and don't go looking for a divorce at the first sign of trouble.

◀◀ **It's a good idea to address the ball with the putter just off the ground so it doesn't catch the ground during the stroke.**

General Technique

Bobby Locke, Billy Casper and Isao Aoki, to pick three players from different generations, would all have had the book thrown at them if there was only one way to putt. The fact that they were three of the best putters of all time fully illustrates that anything goes in putting if it's legal and it works.

Aoki may have been the worst. The manual tells you that the putter head should lie square on the ground; the toe of Aoki's putter hung proudly in the air, as if it was gasping for breath. The manual tells you that the wrists should be firm throughout the stroke; Aoki so cocked his wrists it was as though he was playing a backhand at tennis.

If you saw Aoki on the practice putting green, you would have told him to start again from scratch. Well, you would have if you had told him before he started holing putts from all over the place.

There's one at every club, too, and maybe more than one: golfers who defy conventional putting laws, yet consistently hole out from every area of the green.

To a certain extent then, putting is God-given: that seems to be the lesson here. But for the less gifted among us, there are rules that ought to be followed for consistency in this infuriating area of the sport.

There are perhaps just two basic tenets to putting: the wrists should stay firm throughout the stroke, and the stroke itself should be smooth and rhythmical. The stroke is often compared to the pendulum movement on a grandfather clock and that is probably the best analogy of all. The other thing to remember is that the rest of the body should remain perfectly still throughout the putting stroke. That is not to say that you should be thinking you are a statue and freeze on the spot. Any tension and almost certainly your putting will go to pot. When you are about to stand over a putt, try to relax your body and then concentrate your mind on the ball, moving your arms as if they were that pendulum. Mastered all that? Now the hard part begins – learning to read the greens and the different borrows, as well as coping with the psychology at work.

1 Since a putt spends all its time on the ground there is no need for any wrist action in the stroke. Set up with your eyes over the ball, which should be played just forward of centre in your stance. The shaft of the club and your arms should form a 'Y' shape.

You would think a
psychology degree
would have helped
Tom Watson come to
terms with a decade of
bad putting wouldn't
you? And in a way I
suppose you could say
it did, as it enabled him
to analyze what had
gone wrong and why
he had deteriorated
from being the best
putter from 6ft to
becoming, under
pressure, just about
the worst. But having
broken it all down and
analyzed where it went
wrong, could he put all
the pieces back
together again? Could
the man who won
eight major
championships
between 1975 and
1983 win any after the
magic had gone? Alas
no. A psychology
degree is clearly no
match for the mighty
forces at work
when putting.

2 Keep the clubhead low to the ground as you swing the putter away with your arms and shoulders. Don't hinge your wrists at all and keep your head steady and your lower body still.

3 Always accelerate the putter purposefully through the ball. Never flick at the ball with your wrists to set it rolling. Simply allow it to get in the way of your rhythmical stroke.

Three well-known methods

Given that putting is often considered a game within a game, it is appropriate that a little playing around with the accepted wisdom is allowed here. No-one is going to stand opposite you, studying your grip on the greens, tut-tutting: 'well I'm sorry this will not do,' as they might if they spotted something awry on a shot from the tee.

There's never been a golfer born who has not struggled at some point to get the ball in the hole and experimented as a result with different methods in an effort to find the key. In the end, however, many golfers settle on two of the methods pictured here. The third illustrates putting's boundless possibilities.

The first is the orthodox grip that most players use from tee to green. Perhaps they're working on the principle: heck, it took me long enough to feel comfortable with this method without trying to get used to another one.

Or, alternatively they decided: 'it's working from tee to green, why not on the green as well?'

There's certainly an obvious logic to using an orthodox grip and it represents a good starting point.

What every golfer is after is the feel of the hands being in control of the putter head. Instead of the left index finger forming an interlocking grip, many players find that by placing it over the fingers of the right hand, as in the centre photograph, they can achieve this feel, because the grip is now less rigid. This is perhaps the most popular method of all and the one most used by the top professionals.

The third photograph (far right) illustrates what can only be described as the Langer method. It may look interesting, but be warned; the German only alighted on this drastic solution after three bouts of the putting yips and following experiments with various of other methods.

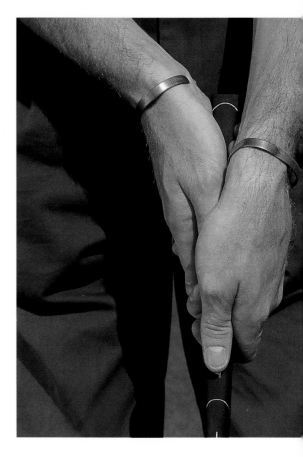

▲ As well as preventing the wrists from breaking down, putting with the left hand below the right levels the shoulders at address and produces a shallower stroke.

Langer has received literally thousands of letters over the years from other sufferers, all enclosing their cure. In the end he came up with his own, although several players, including Sandy Lyle and Roger Davis, have both experimented with it since. Not for long, though. The master remains the ultimate pupil.

▼ **Named after the famous German golfer, the 'Langer' grip locks the left forearm in place and takes the wrists out of the stroke completely. The two-time Masters champion used this grip to help him eliminate the yips in the 1990s.**

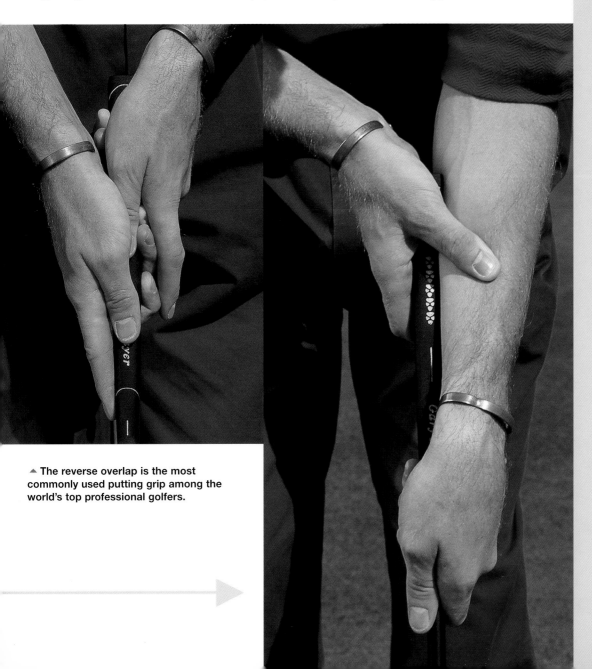

▲ **The reverse overlap is the most commonly used putting grip among the world's top professional golfers.**

Reading greens

Once a golfer has mastered the general technique of putting and settled on a method that promotes feel, the next thing to conquer is how to actually get the ball into the hole. It is one thing to strike the putts correctly and have a good idea of distance. But the ball will still not regularly fall into a small hole unless a player can read the greens.

Sadly, this is a skill gained more by experience than anything else. If you play most of your golf at the same course then you will learn over time the subtleties that exist in those particular greens and master them.

The hard and fast rule to observe is that the golf ball will always follow the laws of Newton. So, if you are putting downhill it is going to travel much faster than in the opposite direction. If a borrow stands between your ball and the hole, then allowances have to be made according to its severity.

The better the greens the more allowance has to be made for borrow. Wet and windy conditions can make quite a difference to putting. If the greens are sodden then the borrows will not have nearly the same effect as if they were dry. As a rough guide, allow perhaps half the borrow you would normally.

If you are putting downwind, inevitably the putt will be quicker than if putting in the opposite direction. The difference can be quite dramatic when the putt is both downhill and downwind. Approach such putts with extreme caution.

Many beginners are always puzzled as to why a top professional studies a putt from all angles, assessing it from behind the hole and also back behind the ball, and occasionally side-on as well.

What they are trying to assess, in addition to the borrows, is the direction of the grain of the grass. If you are studying the putt from behind your ball and the grass looks shiny then this means the grain is with you and the putt will be quicker than if the grass has a matt finish, which means the grain is against.

You'll be pleased to know that greens these days are invariably cut not just in parallel lines but across too, in order to gain a greater consistency and lessen the importance of grain. So don't lose any sleep over it.

▼ **Reading greens well is a skill that comes with experience of playing on a variety of different courses in all weather conditions.**

◀◀ Sam Snead was said to be a poor putter, yet he still managed to win 81 tournaments worldwide during his career.

The putter: your flexible friend

Professionals spend so much time practising these days it is little wonder they indulge in some outrageous experiments. At one tournament I remember watching Fred Couples play an iron shot that eventually finished just short of the green, but in a nasty collar of rough.

What to do now? He could have played a flop wedge shot and watched the ball trickle down towards the flag. He played a rehearsal shot with it, but was clearly worried that the wide face of the wedge would become tangled in the rough before the ball and affect the impact.

1 Once you have determined how much break to allow for on a putt, the difficult part is forcing yourself to aim away from the hole and trust your judgement. Here, the ball will break an enormous amount and Scott has commited to the line and set the ball off well left of the hole.

2 Only experience will teach you how much break to allow for and how hard to strike the ball, but it is a skill that you will acquire fairly quickly.

So instead he got out his Ping putter. Gasps of disbelief went round the gallery. How on earth was he going to putt the ball out of deep rough? Couples had the answer: he was not. Not by a conventional method anyway. He turned the putter on its side so now, rather than having a club with a wide face

swishing through the rough, he had the narrowest one imaginable.

He played the shot to perfection. The edge of the putter collided with the bottom of the ball and it dropped gently on to the green, meandered down towards the flag before falling into the hole.

It was the shot of a master craftsman, of course, but it underlined the flexibility that exists with a putter. It doesn't have to be used just on the putting green. It can be used from a greenside bunker if the face of the sand trap possesses a shallow lip (just remember not to ground it when addressing the ball). Sometimes it is more useful than a seven iron or a wedge from just off the green. I've seen players finish in front of the terrifying Road Hole bunker on the 17th at St Andrews with seemingly no room to negotiate between the trap and the flag. But great golf holes are always designed with an escape route in mind and here the key is the contours of the bunker. The less skilful players ignored them and pitched for the back of the green and settled for a bogey five. But the talented chose their putters, using the contours of the bunker to bring the ball back towards the hole to set up the chance of a par.

The lesson demonstrated here is that, while the putter is the only acceptable club to use on the greens, it is far from the only place where it is acceptable to employ it.

◀◀ **As a rule, it's not a good idea to putt out of the sand, but if the ground is firm and there's no lip, why not?**

Alternative Styles

The putt that won the historic 1985 Ryder Cup at The Belfry, the first time that a team from Europe, as opposed to Great Britain and Ireland, had triumphed against the Americans, was an absolute beauty.

Perhaps you can picture it in your mind's eye: Sam Torrance on the 18th green against Andy North – look at those firm wrists through the stroke and the gorgeous pendulum action and, yards from the hole, there is no doubt that the ball is going to disappear below ground. Yet five years later Torrance had abandoned that stroke, that pendulum movement. He was using a broomhandle putter that should have been banned if the Royal & Ancient had followed its own rules – just how does a broomhandle putter square with the rule that says all clubs should be of a similar likeness? Then again, it is just as well for the Scot that they didn't, for he declared that he would have had to have given up the game if forced to go back to a conventional method.

Alternative putting is nothing new. Another Sam, Snead of that Ilk, was putting with a croquet style towards the end of his career, until the United States Golf Association, the game's ruling body in America, declared it unlawful. No doubt if Snead was playing competitively today he would have filed and won a multi-million dollar lawsuit for loss of earnings and emotional injury.

Once the croquet stance was outlawed, players turned to gripping the club differently. Nowadays many right-handed golfers hold the club using a left-hander's grip: that is, with left hand below right. The elusive thing that they are all trying to recapture is that vital pendulum movement – putting with the left hand below the right is supposed to encourage the hinging of the wrists and a smooth stroke.

With the broomhandle putter, the broomhandle is the pendulum and all Torrance's hands are doing is keeping the pendulum on the right path. Many people, including Tom Watson, think it should be banned for that reason, quite apart from the other, more obvious one. In the R & A's premises at St Andrews they keep a vast selection of all the clubs that have been banned over the years and by far the largest representation is what you might term alternative putters. Putters with wing mirrors, putters with sight lines to look down, croquet putters . . . the list is a tribute to the imagination of man and his powers of invention. It is also a journey into a black hole, to seek a putter that cures all ills. You may as well look for something that enables a soccer player always to put the ball in the back of the net.

▶▶ **Sam Snead's croquet style of putting pushed the boundaries of individuality too far and the USGA eventually made it illegal.**

With all these putters from which to choose, it might be instructive to learn what the best practitioners of the art have selected. Well, I think the two best putters I have seen are Bob Charles and Ben Crenshaw. Charles always used a plain bull's-eye putter that was free of any etchings or markings. And Crenshaw used, nay still uses, a plain blade putter that was given to him while he was at college. Do you think a lesson here might be that putting has more to do with the person than the tool he is using, rather than the other way round, which seems to be how it is promoted by the manufacturers?

◀◀ Sam Torrance is one of several players whose careers – and bank balances – have been transformed by the broomhandle putter.

The yips – golf's deadly disease

◀◀ The yips is a term used to describe an involuntary 'flick' at the ball with the hands during the putting stroke.

▶▶ Bernhard Langer has been one of Europe's top players for several decades yet he has struggled with the yips throughout his career.

It is impossible to believe that there is a more distressing word in the golfer's lexicon than 'yips'. It is a horrible sounding word for a horrible disease and dear old Henry Longhurst's belief – 'once you got 'em you've always got 'em' – has proved sadly true in the case of thousands of golfers. Longhurst, of course, should have known. He so suffered from the yips that he eventually had to give up the game because of them.

Is there any cure for the yips? The television commentator Peter Alliss didn't think so either and it was the crushing onslaught of this condition under pressure that prevented him from ever fulfilling a great talent as a player.

What is it? Basically it is the total breakdown in communication between the brain and the hands. Players have been known to stand over putts unable to take the club back from the ball.

One of the worst sufferers was Harry Vardon, despite the fact that he won the Open on a record six occasions. In his book *How to Play Golf*, he gave a vivid description: 'As I stood addressing the ball, I would watch for my right hand to jump. At the end of two seconds, I would not be looking at the ball at all. My gaze would be riveted on my right hand. I simply could not resist the desire to see what it was going to do. Directly, as I felt that it was about to jump, I would snatch at the ball in a desperate effort to play the shot before the involuntary movement could take effect.'

In the 1988 Open at Lytham, Bernhard Langer, the most famous sufferer in recent times, struck the most marvellous second shot to the 17th, leaving himself with just an 8ft putt for a three. He walked off the green with an eight, having needed four putts from 2ft. When the yips strike, there is nothing you can do.

Langer reckoned that in his case the yips was due to putting on poor greens in Germany as a young man. When he was making a name for himself in his teens, he would quite regularly need 40 putts to complete a round and it was a tribute to his consummate ball-striking and his natural tenacity that nonetheless people still talked of his being a future star.

Yet the Langer story is also one of hope and proof that ultimately Longhurst was wrong. For Langer has had the yips three times and beat them every time. And how he beat them . . . in the 1993 Masters he won the event for a second time and over the notoriously difficult Augusta greens three-putted just once in 72 holes.

In America a couple of years ago a wealthy golfer offered a big cash reward for anyone who came up with something that cured him of the yips. The fellow that suggested giving up the game may have been on to something, but unsurprisingly didn't collect the loot. But of the thousands of remedies suggested one did work . . . and the wealthy businessman happily handed over the cash.

Rules and Etiquette

History of rules

Back then it was all so simple. Back in 1744, when a group of men from the Honourable Company of Edinburgh Golfers got together to draw up a list of governing rules, they felt the necessity to come up with only a handful of regulations. Two hundred and fifty-odd years later and how different things have become. For nearly all that time the rules drawn up by the Royal & Ancient Golf Club of St Andrews have been considered the backbone of the game. Over that time, they have made over 130,000 separate adjudications as people have written in with examples of the game's list of possible variations.

In theory, what we have now are just 34 rules, but in practice each of them brings sheet after sheet of clauses and sub-clauses. They have a life of their own and as new judgements are made, so they change. It is a growth industry.

'They are the equivalent of a complex jigsaw puzzle' states John Glover, former R & A Rules Secretary. states. Hands up if you know all the rules of golf? I bet no more than one golfer in 750 could answer that honestly and still raise their arm.

Certainly not the tournament professionals. They're always falling foul of one obscure rule or another. Hardly a tournament goes by without someone being disqualified for unwittingly breaking the law. Nick Faldo, for example. Given his precise approach to the game, you would think he would know them backwards wouldn't you? Faldo broke two rules in two separate tournaments in 1994 alone. Even in 2001, with so much money at stake, players still don't know the rules. Sergio Garcia lost a tournament in Australia in a sudden death play-off, leaving him to regret a rules infringement in the third round that had cost him two so-vital strokes.

▲ **Although you are allowed to remove loose impediments, if your ball moves as a result, you will be penalized.**

Yet, you've got to have some sympathy for the pros. The most heartbreaking example of all came in 1967 when the Argentinian, Roberto de Vicenzo, birdied the 17th hole to tie Bob Goalby and so force a play-off in the Masters.

That is what happened and in any other sport the act itself would be enough. But not in golf. The player himself has to record all his strokes on a scorecard and when he has signed it, then it becomes a binding contract. De Vicenzo signed for a four on that fateful 17th hole and under the rules of the game the higher score had to stand.

You have to feel sorry for the pros too, in the way that every step they take and every move they make is covered by television and beamed back into the homes of smart alecs who like nothing more than the thought of tripping up the pros.

A few years ago, as Tom Watson and Lee Trevino walked from a green during a tournament, their conversation was picked up by a microphone. Watson was telling Trevino how to cure a fault. A viewer rang in to complain that Watson was giving advice. The complaint was upheld. Watson was penalized.

Ignorance is no defence

And yet for all the importance to the beginner of lessons from a club pro, equally, no golfer should be allowed out on to a course until he has a working knowledge of the rules. That's as much for his own benefit as anyone else's.

John L. Low wrote in 1912, 'Some men have a mutual spirit with the game, and, though they know nothing about the rules of golf, they never have any difficulty in knowing the proper thing to do when some perplexing situation arises.'

What was true in 1912 is palpably not the case now. Say you slice your drive and it comes to rest against a fence that surrounds a clump of trees. Do you just go ahead and play it? Isn't that the proper thing to do? After all, you hit it there. No it isn't. The fence is considered an immovable obstruction and you are allowed to lift and drop without penalty, and now you can play straight for the green.

What if your ball comes to rest against a chopped tree trunk? That's just tough isn't it? Well, actually it isn't. It's considered 'ground under repair' and that's another stroke you've saved.

The pros have raised this kind of interpretation to an art form. They're always looking for line-of-sight rulings from television gantries and the like. Jack Nicklaus once insisted that the rope between two out-of-bounds posts be lowered over his golf ball to determine whether enough of it was in bounds for him to play. It was, and he won the tournament.

So, forget Low and remember Nicklaus's own words, 'Golf was never meant to be a fair game. There is no common justice. There never can be.'

And if you think the rules of golf are unfathomable now, you should have tried learning them 100 years ago. Then it looked as if St Andrews might lose its authority to rule over the game. This was because the sport itself was in turmoil, as most clubs played to rules suitable only for their own terrain. The R & A themselves had a rule that referred to the procedures for recovery from the 'station master's garden.'

Only the Royal Isle of Wight club, with a small nine hole course near Bembridge harbour, framed a set of rules to 'suit all greens', and they received considerable support. So much in fact, that it seemed this modest seaside club might usurp the authority of the R & A themselves.

A game of integrity

A clear example of the once chaotic state of the rules is indicated by the different interpretations that applied if you lost your ball. At St Andrews, it was loss of hole. At the Royal Isle of Wight you hit another from near the place where it was lost and added two strokes. At Hoylake and Westward Ho! it was to go back, losing stroke and distance.

The St Andrews rule was eventually abandoned because it was too harsh, as was the Bembridge law, which left the Hoylake rule as followed today. St Andrews was declared the sole arbiter of the game because there was a general fear that if that authority was handed to the Isle of Wight, the game would polarize into Scottish and English rules. Sadly, the Royal Isle of Wight club no longer even exists. It closed in 1962, and its fairways are now open to the public for picnics. One final point. The most important point of all, in fact. Golf is the ultimate game of integrity. I've seen Peter Baker lose a quarter-final match in the Amateur Championship because he, and he alone, saw his ball move one-quarter of an inch as he addressed his second shot to the 18th hole. Harsh it may seem, but Baker felt obliged to point this out to the referee, knowing that he would have no option but to penalize him the stroke that cost him the game.

In every other sport, it's a case of what you can get away with, but not in golf. Knowing the rules is every golfer's responsibility because he is the sole arbiter of his actions. If people don't know the rules they are liable to break them, and it's a fine line between breaking them deliberately and ignorance. The former are cheats, and those caught have had their lives ruined because their peers believe if they can cheat at golf, they can cheat at anything.

▲ **Tiger Woods and his caddie carefully remove a rake from a bunker at St Andrews, without touching the ball.**

The basic rules of golf

▲ Jean Van de Velde stunned the golfing world when he rolled up his trouser legs and stepped into the burn in front of the green on the 18th hole at Carnoustie in the 1999 Open Championship. However, common sense prevailed and he eventually decided to take a penalty drop instead.

Here are the rules of which you should have a working knowledge before stepping out on to the course.

Rule 7: Practice

After four-putting the 6th green you are quite entitled to try each putt again to see what went wrong, provided there is no-one waiting in the middle of the fairway to play their shots. As you come off the green you can chip your way to the seventh tee if you want, providing again that you are not causing undue delay. What you are not allowed to do is practise on the course prior to playing any strokeplay competition round, nor are you permitted to walk out and test the putting surfaces of any green. If it is a 36-hole competition, no practice on the course between rounds is permitted.

Rule 8: Advice

Your opponent has hit a gorgeous shot, right over the flag, only to see it come up 20yds short of the pin. What are the first words you want to say? If they are, 'Oh, bad luck', then you really are a sport, but most people, I think, would love to say, as they rummage in their own bag, 'What club did you hit?' Please don't say these words. It's a loss-of-hole penalty in matchplay or a two shot penalty in strokeplay competition.

However, if the person who hit the shot is your partner in an event, then by all means go ahead and ask him what club he hit. What advice you are allowed to give concerns the position of bunkers or hazards. You may, for example, have invited your friend to your golf club for the first time. As he's standing on the fourth preparing to hit a 'blind' tee shot, it is as well to inform him that if he goes with the driver in his hands, then he'll be in the ditch that runs across the fairway over the other side of the hill.

Rule 10: Order of Play

When standing on the first tee with your playing partners, there are a number of ways to determine who plays first. Customarily, the player with the lowest handicap will get the game under way,

although you can toss a coin in the air or anything similar that appeals. When you have all reached your tee shots, the player who lies the furthest from the hole plays first and then the second furthest and so on. This continues until the hole is played out. The player who records the lowest number of strokes on that hole will play first, or 'have the honour' as it is termed, on the next tee.

If you drive the ball out of bounds, then you play another ball from the tee after your playing partners have driven off.

Don't worry if you accidentally play out of turn. There is no penalty, but you may be very unpopular.

Rule 11: Teeing Ground

As you stand on the first tee, you go to address your ball and knock it off its tee. 'One,' says one of your amusing partners. Don't be alarmed: it's a joke. You're allowed to tee it up again without penalty. Only if you were making a swing at the ball and you knocked it three inches off the tee would it count as one. Then you've every reason to feel alarmed.

Every club has what is known as the designated tees for that day. There will probably be at least three different tee markers: say, white for competitions, yellow for normal play, red for women. The idea is to tee off within two club lengths behind the tee markers. Most people, of course, tee off in a line with the markers because you don't want to give the course a yard more than you have to. The ball must be placed within the tee markers although you're allowed to stand outside them if you want.

Rule 13: Ball Played as it Lies

From the moment your ball leaves the tee to when you reach the putting green, you must play it from where it lies. An exception is made during the winter months, from 1 November to 30 March in Britain, when you will be able to improve your lie on the fairway, or follow a local rule if one is in operation. If your ball is in the trees you must not break any branches in an effort to get a decent swing at it. The only things you are allowed to move are loose objects, such as acorns or broken twigs, but only if they don't result in your moving the ball.

When in a bunker, you are not allowed to ground the club behind the ball. You are not allowed to smooth down the sand until after you've played your shot and if your ball has landed in a footprint, then sadly that's just tough luck. You are not allowed either to move any loose impediments such as leaves, but you are allowed to move stones if there is a real danger of your striking one on your downswing.

Rules 16 & 17: Putting Green

A ball on the putting green may be lifted and cleaned without penalty. A ball marker is best for this job, but anything is allowed as long as you replace the ball precisely in the spot from where you picked it up.

You can sweep away any loose impediments that lie between your ball and the hole. You may repair any pitchmarks left by inconsiderate people in front. You are not allowed to tap down any spike marks that stand on your route to the hole, however. Confusingly, professionals are allowed to do this.

If you stand a long way from the hole you may either have the flag out or attended by a playing partner, who will remove it before your ball reaches the hole. If you have the flag left in unattended and your ball happens to go in the hole or strikes the flagstick then that's a two stroke penalty. If you are having the flag out make sure it is placed where there is no chance of your striking it with your putt. That would also be a two stroke penalty.

Rule 26: Water Hazards

A water hazard is any sea, lake, pond, river, ditch, or other open water course – whether containing water or not – and should be defined by yellow stakes. A lateral water hazard is one where it is deemed impracticable to drop the ball behind the said hazard, and should be defined by red stakes.

If your ball goes into a water hazard, you drop another ball under penalty of one stroke behind the hazard at the point of entry. What if you're not sure it went into the hazard? The rules say there must be reasonable evidence, or else you have to treat it as a lost ball. If you lose a ball, it means you have to go back and replay the shot from the original spot under penalty of one stroke. If your ball is lost in a lateral water hazard you must play another under penalty of one stroke within two club lengths of the point where the ball entered the hazard. If this is not possible, you can replay your shot from the original position, again adding a one shot penalty.

Rule 27: Ball Lost or Out of bounds

You're allowed to search for five minutes for a ball. If you can't find it within that time, you have to declare it lost and go back and play another from the spot where you hit it under penalty of one stroke. If you drive from the tee into a jungle and there's little chance of finding it, you are allowed to play a provisional ball to save time, but you're not allowed to play a second shot with that ball until the original has been declared lost. A ball is out of bounds if it lies wholly beyond any boundary fence or other area usually determined by white stakes. Under penalty of one stroke you play another from the original spot.

Rule 28: Ball Unplayable

You may declare your ball unplayable at any point on the course except when it is in or touching a water hazard, see above. You have three options. Under penalty of one stroke you may either: drop the ball within two club lengths of where the ball lies, though not nearer the hole; drop the ball behind the point where it lay though keeping the trouble between yourself and the hole with no limit on how far back you can go; trudge back to the spot from where you put yourself in this mess and replay the shot.

▲ As well as knowing how to drop the ball correctly when taking relief or incurring a penalty, you also need to know where to drop it.

Etiquette: what it is and why it is so important

First things first: etiquette is not some obscure French sport. Indeed, the etiquette of golf, its protocol, is among the essential things that every beginner should know before setting out on his first round. As you learn the rules of this game, some of the ways and means will appear illogical and some unnecessary, but etiquette is not among them. At the very least, it will save you hassle from just about every other player you meet.

For a little knowledge in golf can be a very dangerous thing, and a club a lethal weapon in the hands of someone who is not aware that 'fore' is not a polite variation on another four-letter word, but the code that golfers use to indicate that a ball is heading in the direction of another.

You should never play a shot when there is a chance of hitting the players in front, but on courses where fairways are adjacent to one another, you'll occasionally – or perhaps frequently at first! – strike a shot sufficiently off-line that it may disturb the players who are on another hole, in which case you shout 'fore' as loud as you can. Etiquette is all about the general courtesies that one golfer has to show to another to make the game enjoyable. Most instruction books rarely bother about etiquette, preferring to deal in outlandish claims as to how they can have you hitting 300yd drives in a matter of days. But you'll know just how imperative it is from the moment that your first perfectly-struck drive – whether it flies 300yds or not – finishes in the divot left by another. For a golfer, the only thing worse, perhaps, is to wander up to a greenside bunker, mentally prepared to play the shot, only to find the ball in someone else's footprint. Similarly, a green full of pitchmarks is the saddest sight.

You'll probably be already familiar with some aspects of etiquette, even if your only experience of the sport is watching Tiger Woods on television. Not speaking when your playing partner is in the process of hitting a shot, for example. Or not shuffling about on the tee, when someone is about to play. But the most common breach of etiquette is by players who take too long to play the game.

I've dealt with slow play separately, because it really has become the curse of the sport. First, though, some helpful hints on etiquette which will make you a pleasure to play with!

Essential etiquette

The first player to tee off on any hole is the player who has the honour, which is gained by whoever completed the previous hole in the fewest number of strokes. If the scores were the same, the preceding hole is taken into consideration, and so on.

On the tee, always stand opposite to the player who is about to drive off. When you're playing your shot, make sure your partners are opposite you too. If they're behind you, or at right angles to you, there is, at worst, the danger that you may hit them with your club on the backswing, or at best, it can implant the notion in your head that you may hit them, which is the last thing you either should or want to be thinking about.

▲ Leaving your golf bag on the green is the height of bad golfing etiquette.

▲ Always rake a bunker once you have played your shot so that the next person who finds the sand will have a decent lie.

Always make sure the group in front are out of range. A very rough rule of thumb here is to play when they've completed their second shots, and have started walking. But in any case you'll quickly grasp how far you can hit the ball and don't play until they've gone beyond what would be the bounds of your best drive.

When taking a practice swing, it's as well not to take huge divots out of the tees unless you desire your name to appear on a 'Wanted' poster in the head greenkeeper's hut. When in the trees or in a rough area of ground, always clear twigs, pebbles, conkers, or whatever, that you may hit either on your backswing or follow-through. These can be very dangerous both to yourself or someone else. The rules of golf do not allow you to move anything, however, that is still attached to its moorings, so don't get the machete out and start clearing branches that stand in your way or restrict your swing in any way.

On any half-decent golf course, you'll notice a rake next to every bunker. Some golfers seem to think this is merely decoration but it is, of course, to smooth over any footprints, birdprints, dogprints and holes left trying to get the ball out.

Repairing a pitchmark is easy. If your ball has landed on the green from a distance away then it will almost certainly have left one. Pitchmark repairers are available from any professional's shop for a nominal sum and are simple to use.

Two 'never under any circumstances . . .' are pulling your trolley over any part of the green and leaving your bag on it while you putt. Whether carrying your own clubs or using a trolley, always leave them away from the edges of the green. In the winter, you may not be able to pull a trolley if a course is wet, but if you are, don't pull it through any water or within ten yards of any green.

When on the greens, take care not to drag the spikes of your shoes across the putting surface. On well-kept greens this can leave an ugly scar. Spike marks are simply unavoidable on well-prepared surfaces. In big tournaments, you'll often hear professionals who are playing in the afternoon complain about the spike marks left by those who played their rounds in the morning. You can do your bit by treading carefully around the hole and generally not stomping around like an elephant. Leaning on your putter whilst on the green or when picking the ball out of the hole are also habits that are easy to lapse into but ones to avoid.

If one of your playing partners is putting from a long distance away, you could be asked to attend the flag. This involves holding it until the putt is on its way but then removing it before it reaches the hole. Take care that you don't damage the hole in the process of removal. The edges of the holes are easy to deface, and as you've only got an area 4¼ins in diameter to aim at in the first place, the last thing anyone wants is for that small target to be tampered with. This probably sounds like a hefty amount to remember before going on to the golf course, but a lot of it will simply slot into place from the moment you step on to the first tee.

Etiquette

DO
- **Smooth over all footprints and holes left in a bunker.**
- **Repair not just your own pitchmark, but any others you see on a green.**
- **Take care not to damage the edge of the hole, either when removing the flagstick or your ball.**

DON'T
- **Stand behind a player as he is about to tee off.**
- **Take lumps out of the tee with your practice swings.**
- **Ever leave your golf bag or trolley on a green.**

Slow play:
the curse of the game

▲ **With three people reading each putt it's no wonder that some tournaments take an age to complete.**

One thing you will quickly learn in golf is that no golfer ever admits to being a slow player. Calling a golfer slow is tantamount to questioning their parentage. When Severiano Ballesteros was once told at a Tour event that he was being timed for slow play he went bananas, threatening to play in America rather than Europe.

Nick Faldo doesn't think he's slow. Padraig Harrington is the same. The subject has become one of the most sensitive in the sport. By my definition, the above three are all painfully slow, and, sad to say, it is because beginners tend to imitate the superstars, that many of the problems regarding slow play are now with us.

Bernhard Langer is a case in point. He'll carefully place his tee peg in the ground, with the ball on it. He'll have at least a couple of practice swings. Then he'll move 5yds behind the ball. He'll check for the wind strength. He'll come back to the ball. Another couple of looks to check for alignment. Athletes have run 800m in less time than Langer takes to play a single shot.

But at least the German has the perfect excuse. Every time he plays golf, every shot amounts to at least hundreds and often thousands of pounds. He can't afford a single mistake. He's not going out for an enjoyable afternoon's golf, he's going out to make a living. The trouble is, there are just too many golfers who are out for an afternoon's stroll who copy the whole tiresome routine. Cut it out!

We have got to the stage now on some courses where to go round in four hours is considered an achievement. Last year, while on holiday, I was paired up with an American at 3.30pm and the professional told us we had to be in by 6.15pm.

'Should be able to get nine holes in then, shouldn't we?' the American said.

When we'd completed 18 with five minutes to spare, he looked at me as if I'd just forced him to do a marathon. But he was exhilarated too, and he confessed that it was the best that he had played for months. This is what happens when you just enjoy the game, and let it flow, and don't get bogged down by dogma.

I fear we have gone too far now for slow play to ever be eradicated and I'm sure once you're proficient at the game it will annoy you just as much as it does all who love the sport and can take or leave all the periphery.

But here's some basic tips that myself and my friends unconsciously abide by and why our fourball on a Friday afternoon never strays beyond three and a quarter hours.

If you're first or second to tee off, you should be ready, with club replaced in the bag, and bag over your shoulder or hand on trolley, ready to march off the moment your fourth player has completed his shot. This may sound a little unsociable to the last player but it isn't. Remember: you've got at least three hours to talk to them on the golf course, never mind how much time you spend afterwards in the clubhouse.

Again if you're first to tee off, don't delay everyone by marking your score for the previous hole. Do it while someone else is teeing off.

When playing your second shot, don't wait until partner has played before sizing up the wind conditions, how far you've got to go, and what club to play. These are all things that can readily be done while they are playing. Be ready to hit your shot at the appropriate moment.

▸▸ The pace of play at professional golf tournaments can be mind-numbingly slow. The players hate having to continually wait on the tees as it disrupts their rhythm.

▲ America's Phil Mickelson is one of the quicker golfers on Tour and, as such, he is very intolerant of slow play.

Again, on the greens, there is no need to wait for your partner to have finished their putt before reading the line of your own. Of course, there are occasions when you are on the same line, and so you cannot without committing a gross breach of etiquette, but most times you'll find you can, without interrupting the thought processes of your colleague.

If all this sounds as though you're in a race, you'll discover that on the course it's a different matter. Golf, by its very nature, is a slow and time-consuming pursuit. What's causing many of the problems is the people who abuse this basic fact, and it only takes a few golfers of this persuasion to clog up a course and so stretch out a round to five hours, and sometimes even beyond, for everyone.

Few people can concentrate for that length of time, and the most enjoyable rounds of golf that you experience will be ones that take an hour less.

The other prime cause of slow play is an ignorance of the rules of golf. Some clubs have special rules, and the back of the scorecard will usually reveal these, but generally if you're playing with two or three other players, you should wave through any group of two players, or two-ball to give it the golfing term, who are playing behind. Thus you will help to keep the traffic moving. Additionally, if your group falls one clear hole behind the players in front, be it through looking for a lost ball or simply because you are less proficient at the game, then the match behind should be invited to pass.

Scoring

Foursomes, fourball, handicap etc

At the start of this century there were predominantly three forms of the game: there was you against the course; you against an opponent; and you and a friend playing alternate shots against two other players. To that simple equation have now been added many fractions.

Medal play pits you against the course. It is simply a case of adding up how many shots you play on each hole and marking the figure down on a scorecard. Each hole has a par, or the amount of shots that it should be completed in by a professional or an amateur golfer who possesses a handicap of scratch (zero). If the par on each hole adds up to 72 after 18 holes, then it follows that the player with a handicap of scratch has to shoot 72 to live up to his status. Few players get to be that good. In the beginning, you will be more than happy to average two shots above par for each hole. If you average that over three rounds which have been verified by a marker, you would be entitled to a handicap of 36 shots. As you become more proficient your handicap will obviously come down, one day, perhaps down to a single figure, a prized possession indeed.

Sadly, foursomes golf is rarely played these days, except at certain courses such as Brancaster in Norfolk. It is played in the Ryder Cup, however, where the Americans call it scotch foursomes. In foursomes, you and a partner play alternate shots. You hit all the drives on the odd or even numbered holes. Fourballs golf is when you both play your own

ball, and you pit your wits against two opponents doing the same. The best score on each hole by any player wins the hole for his team. That puts them one up. The winners are the pair who get so many holes ahead with one hole less to play. So, if a pair are four holes ahead with three holes to play, they are declared the winners four and three. It is the same in foursomes, although obviously each team only has one ball.

A game of singles matchplay uses the same format, only you are on your own. If you are playing someone off a lower handicap, then he will have to give you shots. You are allowed three-quarters of the difference, with halves rounded upwards. If, for example, you are off 30 and your opponent 20 the difference is 10. Three-quarters of that sum is 7.5, so you will be entitled to eight shots. In foursomes golf, the number of shots given by one side is three-eighths of the difference between each team's combined handicaps.

Where do you take these shots? You will notice on every scorecard a stroke index, in which each hole is graded in terms of difficulty from one to 18. If you are receiving five shots, you take them on the holes with a stroke index of one to five.

The great popularity of the game has inevitably spawned many more formats. There's greensomes, a variation on foursomes, where everybody drives off on every hole, you and your partner select your best drive, and then play alternate shots from thereon in. There's a Texas Scramble, where a team of four selects their best drive, they all play their second shots from there, and then they select their best second shot etc, etc. As you can imagine scores in the 50s in this format are quite common even if you only get one-tenth of the combined handicaps in shots. There's also the shotgun start, where each team begins on a different hole, and so everyone finishes at roughly the same time.

One more that you should know about is the Stableford system. Most club golfers are unhappy with the medal strokeplay format because, although they receive their full handicap allowance, they know that one bad hole can wreck a good card. The more forgiving Stableford system allows for this by awarding points for every hole. If you get an eagle you get four points, a birdie three, a par two, a bogey one, and a double bogey or higher nothing at all. You're allowed seven-eighths of your handicap for this competition.

◀◀ **Seve Ballesteros and Jose Maria Olazabal were almost unbeatable in a foursome in their Ryder Cup matches.**

Match: 31   Time: 12.55
Date: 11 MAY 00
Padraig HARRINGTON (Ire)
Round: 1
Tee: 1

Hole	1	2	3	4	5	6	7	8	9	Out
Metres	376	347	492	404	373	361	162	391	396	3302
Yards	411	379	538	442	408	395	177	425	433	3611
Par	4	4	5	4	4	4	3	4	4	36
Score	6	5	5	4	4	4	2	4	4	38

Signature of Marker.......................

BENSON and HEDGES INTERNATIONAL OPEN 2000

THE BRABAZON COURSE, THE BELFRY

Thursday 11th – Sunday 14th May 2000

10	11	12	13	14	15	16	17	18	In	Total
284	383	190	351	174	498	378	516	433	3207	6509
311	419	208	384	190	545	413	564	473	3507	7118
4	4	3	4	3	5	4	5	4	36	72
3	5	3	4	2	4	4	5	3		71

In 33

Signature of Competitor.......................

◀◀ **A basic error cost Ireland's Padraig Harrington a huge amount of prize money when he forgot to sign his scorecard in the Benson & Hedges International tournament in 2000. He was disqualified when leading by five strokes going into the final round.**

Par, bogey, eagle etc

To the outsider it must often seem that golf has a language all of its own and consequently a conversation between two players in a bar must be bewildering. For example, 'You were putting for an eagle on that hole, but you settled for a birdie. I once saw a man walk off with an albatross there, but I only got a par. Most times I settle for a bogey.' Er, excuse me, what language are we talking here?

As early as the 1880s, a standard score in strokes was being assigned to holes on some courses in England. In 1890, in exasperation at the level of difficulty, Major Charles Wellman, playing at Great Yarmouth, is said to have exclaimed that the standard score of the course was a regular bogey man, referring to the music-hall song that was popular at the time, 'Hush, hush, here comes the bogey man'.

Bogey then became the score that a good amateur should complete for the course. This was always slightly more lenient than par, which became the standard for professionals. At many courses they were one and the same thing, but not always and for some professionals, scoring bogey became second-best, a recognition that they had failed to achieve par.

◀◀ **At most golf courses, eagles of the feathered and golfing variety are very rare indeed . . .**

Over time, then, par became accepted as the score that a good player should achieve, not just over the course of a round but on each hole. If he slipped by one stroke at that hole he had a bogey. Drop two shots and it became a double bogey.

If a player achieves one under par at a hole it is a birdie, two under is an eagle and three under, a very rare occurrence, is accordingly an albatross.

A birdie dates back to 1899 and originates from the American slang word 'bird', which referred to anything wonderful. It was perhaps inevitable that other ornithological references would be used to describe golfing events that were still more sublime.

▲ . . .but not nearly so rare as the sight of an albatross, either in the air or on a par five.

Troubleshooting

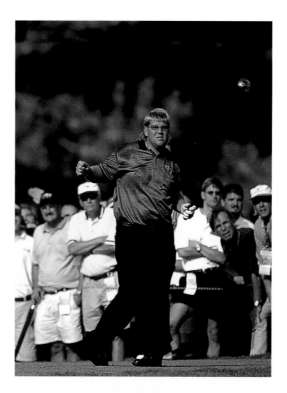

▶▶ John Daly is one of the most charismatic golfers in the game – and he loves an audience to play to.

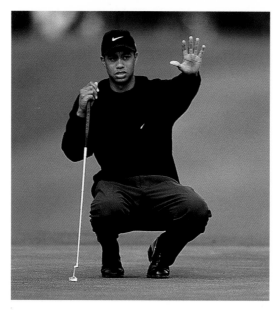

▶▶ Tiger Woods is so focused on the golf course that it is almost impossible to disturb his concentration.

The myths of golf

Like most sports, golf is full of myths. I remember once following John Daly around for a tournament to explore his relationship with the crowd. On every hole they would cry out: 'What d'you hit? What d'you hit?' If Daly had gripped it and ripped it with a six iron he'd say an eight. If it was a four iron he'd say a six. The crowd stood agog: Wow . . . a six iron when I'd use a three wood.

At one point Daly noticed that I had spotted his little white lies and found it amusing. He winked. 'Give them what they want, eh?'

Indeed. And haven't we all done this at some point in the tall tale lounge of the clubhouse? A straight 15ft putt has suddenly become a 25ft putt with three borrows to read. And you always hit the ball 250yds in the tall tale lounge.

It is, of course, totally harmless fun. Well it is if you forget it all by the time you're back out on the course. Unfortunately, many people don't and if there is one thing that gets more people into more trouble on the course, it is inflating their idea of their own capabilities. You see it time and time again.

Perhaps the biggest myth, though, is the time-honoured advice to keep your head still. You see this in virtually every instruction book. When you swing the club . . . make sure you keep your head still. When you're standing over a 12ft putt . . . make sure you keep your head still. For the record: it is a physical impossibility to keep your head still while you complete the golf swing. It is undesirable even to try it when you're putting. It increases tension and this is the one thing you don't want while you are on the greens.

The mental game

As I have said before, golf is a game played in inches and the most important of all are the inches that separate your ears. What is going on in that space will determine your fate on the golf course every time. If you are upbeat and your frame of mind is positive, you're more than halfway to a good score.

The importance of the mental game has become much more apparent in recent years. Many top professionals now regard the sports psychologist as an important part of their armoury. The genial Irishman David Feherty used to rely so much on his psychologist Allan Fine that he was even prepared to meet him at 6 o'clock one morning on Waterloo Bridge in London because it was the only time that Fine could fit him in!

You don't need to be looking up some Harley Street addresses, however, to feel the benefits from an improved mental approach. Just appreciate how important the mental game is. Here are the key points to a strong mental game:

1. Visualize your shot: before you play each shot you should have a mental picture of how you want the ball to fly and what you want to achieve.

2. Don't dwell on bad shots: how many times have you heard a player say, 'I talked myself into that shot.' It's true, too. Cluttering up your mind with the seven iron shot you put in the water will wreck the next one you play and will end up wrecking your card as well. Forget it. Tell yourself that anyone can hit a shot in the water. Hell, Severiano Ballesteros once lost the Masters by duffing a four iron into the water at the 15th.

Dwell instead on all the seven iron shots that you have struck right out of the middle of the club. If you have a particular shot on your course that causes you problems, or a particular hole, then analyze it when you get home. Is there another strategy you could try? Am I thinking hard enough? Am I doing enough to convince myself while walking up to the tee that I can play the right shot?

◀◀ Undoubtedly the best golfer in the mental stakes was Jack Nicklaus. Is it any coincidence that he was also more successful than anyone else? Even now, just watch the Golden Bear in action and the powers of concentration he employs. 'When Jack was at his best, it was almost scary how well he concentrated,' says Lee Trevino. 'He could talk himself into playing any shot well, no matter how difficult it appeared.'

Hazards

1. The rough

Throughout this book, the point has been made that golf is a game for all and rarely discriminates in favour of one physical specimen. Playing from the rough, however, is the big exception. Here, if you're as strong as a gorilla with forearms like Popeye, it has to be said that you're at an advantage.

A lot of municipal and pay-as-you-play courses have little rough because they slow down play and, in any case, most high handicappers or newcomers to the sport don't want to be up to their knees in the rough stuff on every other shot.

On a championship course, the rough will come in various shapes and sizes. The first cut of rough, usually known as the semi-rough, lets you off lightly. Indeed, as far as the average golfer is concerned, you can often have better lies in the semi-rough than on the fairway since there will be a cushion of grass under the ball. The top players are less happy because this induces what is known as the 'flying lie', where the grass comes between the blade of the club and the ball, causing it to fly further as there is no chance of imparting spin. The average player is delighted, of course, with anything that causes the ball to fly further.

A tee shot that strays further off-line deserves to be punished with a second cut of rough and this you will find, usually 15yds or so off the fairway. Here your fate is in the lap of the gods and your response to it depends entirely on your lie.

If you can hardly see your ball, then clearly you need to use a sand wedge to chop the ball just back on to the fairway. But even if it is visible, do not be too greedy. Look at the grass all around the ball and determine how much this is going to interfere with

clubhead speed. If you think it will interfere too much, you need a lofted club. If you've struck lucky, then go with a six or seven iron. Unless you name is Tiger Woods resist any temptation to try anything fancy. Remember that the object of the exercise is damage limitation, so accept a bogey and leave it at that.

2. Trees

Some courses have hardly any rough – Augusta National is a case in point. Woburn in Bedfordshire doesn't have that much either. Both rely on woodland to protect their holes and what a good job it does.

There's nothing nicer than playing a course like Woburn or Wentworth that has been cut from mature woodland. However, apart from an expanse of water, there is probably nothing more intimidating to the mid-handicap golfer. For six holes they will never miss a fairway. Then he comes to the seventh, where the fairway is framed by trees on either side and suddenly the slice that only comes out at such times is there again.

The key to conquering such fear is to focus on a spot in the middle of the fairway and cut the trees from the mind. By all means admire the flora on your walk around the course, but once you are standing over your ball you should be thinking to yourself: 'Trees? What trees?'

However, there will be times when your ball disobeys your every urging and decides to go for a rummage in the woodland. Once again your main task is to exercise damage limitation. What if there's a small gap and if you can thread the ball through it you can advance the ball 120yds rather than coming out sideways? Realistically, how many

▲ The biggest mistake amateurs make when playing out of the rough is trying to hit a long iron. In most cases, the best approach is to simply get the ball safely back in play.

One of the greatest shots from the rough was played by Arnold Palmer in the 1961 Open at Royal Birkdale. Palmer had pushed his tee shot on the 16th in the final round into heavy rough and a machete looked about the only club to use. There were gasps from the watching spectators when Palmer called out for a six iron. Palmer nearly swung himself off his feet as those massive forearms powered the club through the Birkdale scrub to propel the ball 140yds on to the green. Palmer got his par and went on to win the title by one stroke.

times out of ten do you think you can pull it off. Once? Twice? Forget it.

Think about it this way. You still can't make the green, but you will have a 30yd shot instead of one of 150yds. Clearly you're more likely to rescue a shot from the former situation, but it's far from certain and nowhere near enough to outweigh the damage if you fail to make it through that gap. Imagine if the ball hits a tree? It could you plunge you further into the woodland and you would be looking at an horrendous score. It is essential to think sensibly and clearly and not get overtaken by dreams of glory.

If the shot requires you to keep the ball under branches, then take a straighter-faced club. You will need to position the ball further back in your stance, and remember to swing slowly and smoothly. It's very easy to swing quickly and hit behind the ball and move it about 18ins.

One further important note: take great care when playing out of trees. A ball that ricochets off a tree is a dangerous weapon, so make sure there is no-one standing nearby who is in danger of being struck. If there is a danger of the ball flying back and striking you, then for heaven's sake take a safer option. You're not playing for the Open!

▲ There is nothing wrong with admiring the beauty of the trees, but it's best not to focus on them as you stand over the ball.

Hazards

3. The fairway bunker

It's quite easy to spot the player who feels intimidated from the moment he steps into a fairway bunker. Just watch the swing: what had hitherto been smooth and rhythmical is now quick and jerky. They will either strike the sand first and the ball will subsequently squirm its way out of the bunker or they will thin the shot, blasting the ball into the bunker's face.

Actually, if the lie is good, this is a fairly straightforward shot. With the one proviso that you can't ground your club, you should play this like any other long iron shot. You will lose some distance so what would be a six iron shot off the fairway now becomes a five iron.

Unless you are a good golfer, or feel confident over this shot, it is sensible to take nothing straighter than a five iron.

1 From a clean and level lie there is very little difference between the fairway bunker shot and a normal shot from the grass. However, to avoid catching the sand before the ball, stand a little taller at address.

2 Keep your lower body as steady as possible as you make your swing and keep everything as smooth as possible to avoid any sudden changes of direction that could cause you to lose height.

3 Avoid dipping into the ball at impact as this is likely to lead to you hitting the sand well behind the ball. The end result? A shot that flies much shorter than you expected.

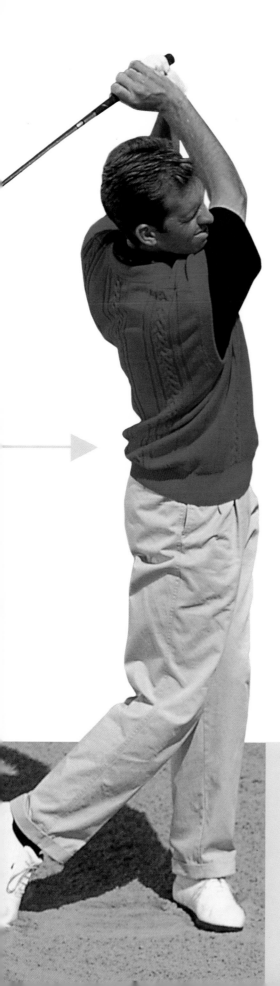

In any case, it would have to be a fairly shallow-faced bunker or your ball placed well back in the sand trap for you to be able to use even a five iron. Don't fall for the sucker punch of being too greedy and failing to get out of the bunker. If ever there's a feeling that you've just carelessly frittered away a shot, it is when you gamble in a fairway bunker and lose.

4. Playing off a path

In most instances you will not have to play off a path since it is classed as an immovable obstruction and you are therefore allowed to drop your ball off it, without penalty, as long as you are no nearer the hole.

On many older courses, however, paths and roads have been declared an integral part of the course (the local rules on the back of the scorecard will usually specify if this is the case) and you will have to play the ball as it lies.

Again, this is a fairly straightforward shot, and your approach should not be that much different to playing off the fairway. Aim to take the ball cleanly.

Playing off a path will undoubtedly cause one or two minor scratches to the sole of your club so be warned. Of course you may decide you don't want to risk damage to the bottom of your club and declare the ball unplayable, in which case you can drop off the path or road under penalty of one shot.

4 As with any other swing, you must finish with your weight on your front foot and your right shoulder facing the target if you want to generate plenty of distance out of a fairway bunker.

Hazards

5. Out of bounds

There aren't many worse feelings in the game than walking up to your ball and discovering that it is has finished a few yards the wrong side of the out of bounds line. You feel as though you've just thrown two shots away to the course.

Out of bounds is determined usually by boundary fences or walls, and by white stakes. Again the intimidation factor is at play here. If your normal shot is a little slice and there is a boundary wall on the right and the wind is blowing in that direction, then a feeling of helplessness and a dread certainty of what is about to happen can set in.

Once more the key is to swing slowly and not thrash at the ball. It doesn't matter if your ball goes 20yds less down the fairway – the key is to always find the fairway.

Remember that your ball is still in bounds, even if you have to stand out of bounds to play it, and that your ball is allowed to be out of bounds for its entire flight, indeed even when it lands and hops, skips, and jumps, as long as when it finishes its journey it is back in bounds.

A perfect example of this came in the regional qualifying round for the Open Championship at Blackwell in 1994, when at the eighth hole Wayne Stephens's drive sailed over the boundary fence. So did his provisional ball. He was now looking at a nine until he spied a lovely white object in the middle of the fairway and upon identification realized that his first ball had pitched on the road outside the boundary fence and bounced back in bounds. Instead of a nine Stephens got a four. He went on to shoot 63, which shaved three strokes off the previous course record.

▲ Tour pro Stephen Bottomley takes a penalty drop at the British Masters, at Collingtree.

6. Water

The first thing to stress with regard to water hazards is how important it is to know the rules. Generally, a water hazard is defined by white stakes and you have to drop your ball behind it if you've finished in one, under penalty of one stroke.

However some water hazards are defined by red stakes and these are lateral, which means that you are allowed to drop at the point at which your ball entered the water. You can see the fear in some people's eyes when they are confronted by a water hazard. They'll let out an expletive and shout, 'How the hell am I going to get across that!' It is at this point that you know that they are not.

It is important to appreciate that water is there to intimidate and it can often do so against the very best players. In the 1989 Ryder Cup at The Belfry, eight out of the 12 singles matches went to the final hole where one of the players proceeded to find the water in no less than five of the games. In another, between Ballesteros and Azinger, both players found the water!

If there really is no chance of your getting across, then you should play safe and opt for the bail-out route that is usually available. If there is no bail-out route then clearly you are playing a golf course that was designed for a player of a higher standard. The one glaring mistake that most players make is to swing too quickly. In fact you should be swinging slower than normal, to make absolutely sure that you strike the ball correctly and so clear the hazard. If you're playing over water to a green, then take a club more than you would normally select. Remember: as you contemplate the shot, you should be thinking 'slow', not 'oh no!'

▲ **Because so many tee shots find the water at the treacherous par three 17th hole at TPC of Sawgrass, there is a special drop zone.**

Deliberate slice and fade

All right, let's get the jokes over with: what do I want with a deliberate slice when I have one with every shot? My problem is that I'm trying to get rid of a deliberate slice.

There will be times when your view of the green or your desired spot on the fairway is blocked out by trees or some other object and that, in order to make the putting surface, you will need to fade the ball, or, in extreme cases, slice it.

In such a case you need to open your stance with the ball positioned an inch or so further back than normal. Instead of an imaginary parallel line in front of

1 To curve the ball from left to right in the air, aim your feet and body on the line you want the ball to start but aim the clubface at the target.

2 Commit to swinging the club back along the line of your feet and body to ensure that your swing path is from out-to-in.

3 Swing back down to the ball on the same path as the backswing so that the clubface cuts across the ball at impact creating the left-to-right sidespin.

your feet pointing towards the target, the line should now point to the left of it. This will make you take the clubhead back on a much steeper angle and the clubface will be slightly open at impact, giving you a fade. Of course if you require a slice then both movements need to be exaggerated. Your stance needs to be very open and you should be able to feel that the clubhead is travelling on a wider arc than your normal swing path.

Clearly this is a shot that isn't going to come off the first time you try it. You're going to have to spend some time on the practice ground and work on the principles, but it is certainly a useful weapon to have. And who knows: once you've learned how to hit a deliberate fade, you'll realize what you were doing wrong to cause that all too familiar slice!

4 For maximum effect, hold the clubface open through impact by preventing your right forearm from rotating through the ball and, in turn, squaring the blade of the club.

Lee Trevino deliberately fades the ball with virtually every shot he hits. The Mexican plays with an open stance and aims for the left side of every fairway knowing that his fade will bring the ball back into the middle. In fact, it is one of the least destructive shots that a golfer can play. When the ball hits the ground it has sidespin and so doesn't travel far. A player whose natural shot is a draw has to live with the fact that he hits it with topspin and so the ball rolls forever . . . and sometimes into trouble.

Deliberate draw and pull

These two shots are a mirror image of those described on pages 162–3, but now you need a closed stance, and that imaginary parallel line in front of your feet should point to the right of the target. The ball should be slightly further forward in your stance because you want the clubface closed at impact.

On the backswing you should be flatter than normal and the club should be inside your usual swing path. Again a little practice is essential here.

This is a shot that is easy to overcook, and do bear in mind that it can lead to disastrous results – whereas a slice will land softly, a ball that is a draw

1 To draw the ball from right-to-left in the air, first aim the clubface at the target, then aim your feet and body to the right on the line you want the ball to start.

2 As with the fade, once you've adjusted your alignment, you must commit to swinging along the line of your body.

3 Just as a tennis player will rotate his or her forearms powerfully through impact to produce that enviable top spin on the ball, so you must do the same to create the right-to-left flight.

will hit the ground running. Of course if you are blocked out by trees on the left of the fairway and the green is miles away then a deliberate draw can be spectacularly successful and gain you yardage you hadn't thought possible.

But it is as well to be aware of the pros and cons of the deliberate draw and a lot of very good players whose natural shot is a fade, including Colin Montgomerie, steer clear of it for the most part because they have difficulty controlling it.

4 Compare the position of the forearms and the clubface with the finish position on the previous page 163. Here the grooves on the club are pointing more towards the ground, whereas on the fade, they aim more towards the sky.

Restricted swings

Restricted backswing

If ever a shot depended on rhythm it is the one where the backswing is restricted. All too often the player, in an effort to compensate for a loss of power, will try to accelerate quickly through to impact, succeeding only in disturbing the rhythm and hitting behind the ball with disastrous consequences.

Another common fault is looking up too quickly to see whether a shot has been successfully executed. Any player who looks up too quickly

will do so to discover that his efforts have ended in embarrassing failure.

The thing to concentrate on here is rhythm. Making a good contact with the ball is all-important, so the key is to make sure the restriction to your backswing doesn't interfere. You can do this by ensuring that the tempo of your swing is correct. Play the ball toward the back of your swing to maximize your chances of striking it cleanly and hinge your wrists early in the backswing.

1 When your backswing is restricted, set your weight more towards your front foot so that you can pick the club up steeply and avoid the tree. Play the ball towards the back of your stance to maximize your chances of striking it cleanly.

2 Make a couple of practice swings before playing the shot for real. Hinge your wrists early in the backswing to take the width out of the shot.

3 Hit down positively on the ball with a sharp descending blow. Don't quit on the shot and make sure that you accelerate the cubhead through impact.

Restricted follow-through

The first question to ask when the follow-through is restricted is whether you are going to damage either yourself or your club. It could be that your hand is going to collide with a branch or tree after impact, and the shaft of the clubhead as well.

Unless you are playing in a vitally important match, if there is any danger of either of these things happening, it is wise to declare the ball unplayable and take a drop under penalty of one shot.

Such is the force of the swing that if the middle of the shaft collides with the branch of a tree after impact, there is every chance it will snap. This happened to Brett Ogle in the 1994 Hawaiian Open and he almost lost an eye as the shaft's jagged edge came back towards him.

If the follow-through is restricted by a bush, however, or something softer, then don't let it put you off. Just swing normally. What happens to your follow-through after impact will not affect the ball.

1 When the restriction is on your follow-through and not your backswing, you can set up normally to the ball without amending your address position at all.

2 Once again, you can go ahead and make your normal backswing. The important part on this shot is the downswing.

3 The shaft of the club can snap easily if it hits the tree – and so can your wrists. This is one of the few times where it's permissible to ease up a little through impact. Swing softly through the ball and restrict yourself to an abbreviated follow-through.

Where to practise

For some golfers, of course, this chapter is completely and utterly irrelevant. Many never see a practice ground from one year to the next and their idea of a driving range is a selection of cars.

Practice doesn't have to be unspeakably boring. It doesn't have to rank alongside doing the washing up, cleaning the car or mowing the lawn. It can be useful and interesting. Honestly.

The key is to practise with a purpose. Don't go without an idea in your head and then hit balls aimlessly. Whilst in the car on the way to wherever you're going to practise, make a mental list of the three things which you would most like to improve and work on those diligently. Limit yourself to maximum of two hours.

The place where most people practise is the local driving range and these have improved greatly as the demand has risen in recent years. Ten years ago a typical range was run down with poor teeing mats and even poorer golf balls.

You should now be able to find one locally that is swish and modern. The best have miniature greens with flags indicating 50yds, 75yds, 100yds etc. Rather than just being flat and boring they've been landscaped. A small fee will get you a bucket of balls; they can do your golf a power of good and represent excellent value.

Most of the traditional clubs have very limited practice facilities. Some of the more recently-built establishments will have a practice bunker from which you can play as well as a practice green to which you can chip. Often you can use these for a small sum, even if you are not a member.

Some of you will become sufficiently hooked on the game to install a private net at home into which you can smash golf balls to your heart's content. This, to me, has always seemed unspeakably boring.

Another way of practising your long irons and woods at home is with a practice golf ball which is made of plastic and full of holes, making it fairly difficult to damage anyone or anything.

Patio owners can check a few things by looking at their reflection in the glass of their patio doors. By facing the glass, you can check that the ball is positioned just inside your heel. By completing your backswing you can make sure you are not taking the club back beyond the horizontal.

Now stand side on to the glass and check your address position. Are you standing 'tall' to the ball, but with your knees flexed and your body relaxed? Are your hands far enough away from your body? Now swing the club back: is the shaft pointing down an imaginary straight line to the target? When you swing through, check that your finishing position leaves you face on to the glass.

There. Not so boring after all was it?

Essential practice drills

There's no getting round the fact that bringing your long game up to a proficient level is going to require a fair amount of work. Here are six practice drills to help you get the most out of your woods and long irons:

1 Tee the ball up with your long irons. Now I know you're not allowed to do this when playing on the course, but the thing that intimidates most players about the long irons is their lack of loft. They attempt to compensate by trying to scoop the ball into the air. By putting the ball on a tee you're providing some

▲ **Regular trips to the driving range are great for your game, but only if you practice effectively when you're there.**

loft and so now you can concentrate on the smooth and rhythmical tempo that is so vital to good iron shots. Watch the great long iron players like Lee Westwood and Ernie Els. How often, as they strike another one iron down the fairway, have you said to yourself it's like shelling peas? The secret is they don't swing any faster with a one iron than they would with an eight iron.

When you've mastered playing the shot off a tee you can progress to playing them off the grass or from a tee mat.

2 Sweeping to success. Sam Snead, one of the great drivers of all time, said that the thing he concentrated on when hitting his tee shots was the feeling that he was sweeping the ball off the tee. This remains one of the great tips. Just try it. Get that picture in your mind of a sweeping action through the ball. This will encourage you to swing freely in the hitting area.

3 Check your alignment. This is best done with the help of a friend or practice partner. Line up to the target. Now ask your colleague to place a club so that it is lined up against your toes. It should be pointing directly at the target if you're aligned properly. It isn't? You're hardly alone. Many players are absolutely astonished at how far out their alignment is when they do this simple exercise. If you're one of those players, it can feel really strange when you set-up correctly, pointing towards the target, but persevere. Retrain your muscles so that they're focused properly, and practise a few shots at the driving range, remembering to leave that club on the ground in front of your toes.

4 Always have something to aim at. A driving range is good in this case because there are targets at which you can aim. But if you are in an open field or on the club's practice ground, find a spot in the great blue yonder upon which you can focus. Better still, pace out 200yds and stick an umbrella or something in the ground. Hitting balls without a target makes it hard to concentrate and you can easily lapse into the sort of faults that you came to the practice ground to eradicate.

5 Left shoulder visible. One of the most common faults among golfers is the failure to coil properly during the backswing, thus losing a great deal of power and distance. Here's an easy way to check that you are turning your upper body on the backswing. When you get to the top, the point of your left shoulder should be over the ball. If it is, then your upper body is coiled nicely and you are in the correct position to gain distance and power through the ball.

6 Struggling with your rhythm and tempo? You see it all the time. A nicely controlled backswing. An ungainly lash at the ball. Or an ungainly backswing, followed by an ungainly lash at the ball. With good tempo and rhythm a golfer can compensate for many other faults.

One way of improving this side of your game is to practise with a half swing, that is, take the club back to the nine o'clock position and then on through to the three o'clock position. This discipline promotes smoothness of rhythm so give in to it. After a few minutes try swinging the club back to your normal position using the same key thoughts.

▲ **Picking a high target to aim at behind the green is always a good idea, but you won't often have a backdrop as spectacular as this.**

Warm-Up Exercises

Playing golf by itself may not get you fit, but it can certainly leave you armchair-bound. A round of golf lasts a few hours and in that time the back, the knees and the feet all get a hammering every time you play.

The back in particular, of course, takes most of the strain. The number of golfers who suffer from ailments in the lumbar area are legion. Even the best golfers are not immune; indeed they are some of the worst sufferers.

If you're hitting golf balls all day every day then it is inevitable that such repetition is going to take its toll on muscles and ligaments. Fortunately, none of us have to subject ourselves to such a regimen.

There are some things you can do to avoid back problems. For instance, when you go to the boot of the car to take out your clubs, the temptation is to yank them out, not thinking of the strain you are putting on the lower back. Thousands of golfers have

⏶ One of the biggest mistakes you can make is to tee off without first warming up your muscles. Always make the time for a few gentle stretches.

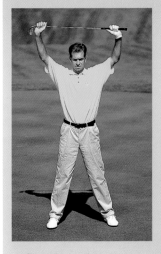

▲ Stretch out those stiff muscles in your shoulders and upper back by holding a club above your head and raising it slowly and gently.

done this only to find a muscle give way before they have even struck a ball, spoiling their afternoon's pleasure. The irony is that if you were lifting a 30lb weight out of the boot, you would take great care – a golf bag is the same weight and so, of course, demands the same amount of attention.

Similarly, don't just step on to the first tee and lash at the ball while all your muscles are still cold. That's a real recipe for disaster. Here we've come up with some key exercises to help you protect those parts of the body that the golf swing puts under the most strain. They are best completed at home before your round of golf. Try doing them daily if you can. They will take no more than 15 minutes at most and will leave you healthier and fitter to play your favourite sport.

▲ This is a particularly good exercise for loosening up your back and shoulders and it will also remind you of how to coil your upper body correctly in the swing.

Distance judgement

Using yardage charts and sprinklers

Many old professionals consider that some of the art of the game has been taken away in recent years with the development of artificial aids to determine how far a player has to the green.

Certainly a little of the skill has been taken out. If you're standing right in the middle of the fairway with the wind blowing a little, debating which club to take, and all you've got to go on is your mind's eye, then clearly distance judgement is more difficult than if you possess a yardage chart which tells you exactly how far you need to hit the shot.

Yardage charts are an invaluable aid to any player who knows exactly how far they hit every club. It enables them to plot their way round the golf course; how to avoid hitting into a ditch or bunker off the tee; and what club to take to find the middle of the green. There really is no excuse for under or overclubbing.

Or is there? There are a number of ways in which a golf architect can make a mockery of a yardage chart and we shall deal with them overleaf.

Most courses now have some sort of yardage indicators on the course. It may be a stake or a small bush at the 150yd mark. Some courses in Great Britain, and nearly every course in America, will also have the yardage printed on a selected number of fairway sprinkler heads.

These are a wonderful aid, but before you go out, do make sure you establish whether they are measured to the front or the centre of the green. On a course where they have large putting surfaces it can make a huge difference; you may find yourself on the fringe of the green with a very long shot to the pin despite your seemingly perfect approach shot.

Of course in the professional world they take yardages very seriously. Many caddies will go out 48 hours before the start of a tournament armed with a measuring wheel and, knowing roughly where their man will hit the ball, they mark off points so they know exactly how far the player will have to the flag.

This may seem to be taking things to the extreme when, on the courses the pros play, the yardages are on virtually every other sprinkler head. But think of it this way: they know how far they hit each club almost to the yard; a yard each way can make the difference between a holed putt or a miss; one stroke can mean a great deal of money. In this light, it no longer seems so extreme.

Colin Montgomerie tells a very amusing story on this subject which he insists is true. It happened in the 1991 Ryder Cup at Kiawah Island when he was partnering that well-known perfectionist, Bernhard Langer, in the foursomes.

It was Monty's turn to drive off on one hole and he duly found the middle of the fairway. As they assessed the second shot that Langer had left, the German called out to Montgomerie, who was standing a few yards away. 'What yardage have you got from that sprinkler head?' Langer asked. Monty looked and consulted his yardage book. '170,' he said. Langer replied, with a touch of impatience:

'Yes, but is that from the front of the sprinkler head or the back?'

▲ **Many golf courses now have yardages to the green written on sprinkler heads and plaques in the fairway.**

▶▶ **A key part of a caddie's job is to walk the course before a competition to familiarize himself with all the different yardages.**

Quick tip

Nearly every golf club has yardage charts, but they vary enormously and many players make the big mistake of turning immediately to hole one and wondering why their opening iron shot is on the front of the green when the book said they had 150yds to go and they normally hit a seven iron that distance. Some yardage charts have measurements to the front of the green, that's why, and a cursory look at the opening page would have revealed this fact. So take care to swot up on this information before you start your round and not when you're cursing over a 50ft putt the length of the first green.

Using your eyes

As I said, there are a number of ways in which the golf architect can render a yardage chart worthless, and any decent course will have a couple of holes that duly do this. The trick is to be able to spot them on the tee.

One potential troublemaker is the par three with an elevated tee set far above the green. The hole measures 160yds. So what club to use. Do you take the club with which you normally propel the ball 160yds? If you did, however, you would almost certainly be hacking out of the rubbish behind the green for your second.

Elevated tees foreshorten any hole, and the higher up you are in relation to the green, the less club you need to take. If the elevation is 30–40ft then you will need two or even three clubs less than you would normally hit.

After that salutary experience you move on to a long par four, slightly uphill this time. You've got 140yds to go. Now you need one club more than usual and again, if the gradient is steep then you may need two or three clubs more.

Flat par fours can be dull and boring, but a good architect will try and liven them up in some way. He may put two bunkers in left and right at the front of the green. Beware of this, because it invariably has the effect he's looking for of foreshortening the hole.

If the yardage chart says 160yds and you can't believe it's that far, then disbelieve the evidence of your own eyes.

The other person who can make a mockery of the yardage chart, of course, is Mother Nature. If the wind is howling, then 150yds becomes a figure for negotiation, with obviously more club needed if you are playing into the wind and less if it is in your favour.

The wind can play immense tricks with a golf ball. The trick is to try not to hit it high so as to lessen the influence of the wind.

The professionals are great to watch in this instance. As I mentioned earlier in this book, keep your eye on a terrific wind player like Tiger Woods. It is worth repeating that he won't be frightened of hitting a little knockdown seven iron 130yds if it means he can keep it under the wind and so control it.

A firm contender for the greatest round of golf played in inclement conditions was Greg Norman's second round in the 1986 Open at Turnberry. Most players were thrilled if they came in with a score within touching distance of the stringent par of 70. Norman shot 63, and went on to win the event by five shots. No less a luminary than Tom Watson called it 'the finest round of golf in an event in which I have been a competitor'.

◄◄ Even the world's top golfers need a second opinion every now and then. Here, Tiger Woods' caddie Steve Williams helps him with the line of a tricky putt.

The wind factor

Golf can be plain contradictory at times. The New Course at St Andrews is one of the oldest courses in Britain. If you want to hit the ball left, for instance, you aim right. Similarly, if you want to play your best golf when playing into the wind then don't hit the ball so hard.

Golf in the wind can be an interesting experience for someone who is used to playing in relatively calm conditions. I once had an American friend who came over to stay. At his place, well, if he had 160yds to go it had to be a six iron.

So I took him to Royal Birkdale and yes, the wind was blowing a storm. The first time he had 160yds to go we were playing downwind and he hit a wedge over the green. The next time was into the gale. He took a three iron and struck it right out of the 'sweet spot' to finish 20yds short of the green.

That's what the wind can do. It can mock all our best-laid plans.

Tiger Woods has become one of the best wind players of his generation through sheer dedication. When he first played in the Open at St Andrews he would hit every shot high and the wind would mock him. Now watch him. If the circumstances demand it he will think nothing of using a seven iron to propel

◀◀ **Tiger Woods has worked hard to become a more versatile player and he is now one of the world's best wind players.**

▶▶ **Reduced gravity enabled astronaut Captain Alan Shepard to hit the ball over 200 yards one-handed with a make-shift club on the moon.**

the ball 130yds, if that is the club he needs to swing slowly and keep everything under control.

If you're playing a tee shot into the wind, then tee it up a little lower than you would normally, but don't go digging for it because you will do just the thing you most wanted to avoid – sky the ball up into the air.

Everyone loves hitting tee shots downwind, watching the ball sail for miles. In this instance, tee the ball up a little higher, but don't swing any faster. If the wind is very strong then consider a three or even four wood, because clearly the thing you want most of all is the ball to stay in the air.

The wind that most players dread is the one that blows over the shoulder. If it's into your face you can hold steadfast against it, but when it's over your shoulder, it can affect your balance. It's a good idea here to widen your stance by a couple of inches, but again: a slow swing. This cannot be stressed enough.

Playing into the sun and rain

Initially, these would appear to be two extremes: the pleasure of playing golf on a sun-kissed day, and on the other hand the utter misery of trudging round 18 holes getting soaked to the skin. In reality, it is not all plain sailing on one hand, and the other doesn't have to be a completely miserable experience.

▲ **Playing in the rain isn't so much of a hardship – if you're properly attired, that is.**

Playing into the sun inevitably invites you to lift your head too early to try to spot where the damn ball has gone. Of course all that happens is you end up squinting into a yellow blur. What makes it worse is that if you've lifted your head too soon you won't even have the satisfaction of watching a good shot to comfort you.

The best way to combat this is to ask one of your playing partners if he will kindly do the honours. If you're playing on your own . . . the best advice is to concentrate on making sure you hit a good shot and, well, it won't matter if you haven't seen it then because it will have gone down the middle won't it?

Playing with a cap or a visor can obviously help to cut down the glaring rays of the sun, although many people find them more of a distraction than a help if they're not used to them.

Playing with a cap is more than useful if it's bucketing down. So is a good rain suit. And waterproof shoes.

Ensure you have three or four small towels with you to enable you to keep your grips as dry as you can. Once these become wet, you've really no chance of playing well, no matter how nicely you're swinging, so pay extra care to this. An idea is to hang one under your umbrella so it is easily accessible to dry both your hands and clubs.

This is another instance when swinging slowly and smoothly can bring great dividends. Concentrating harder can also help to combat the depressing effects of the weather.

▶▶ **Wearing a visor will help you in both the sun and the rain.**

There can often be as much as two clubs difference between hitting shots on a sunny day and one filled with rain. In the sun, the ball will travel further through the warm air and, if there has been a succession of nice days, will obviously roll further on the baked earth once it lands. In the wet, the ball clearly won't be going anywhere once it squelches down, so take a club more than you would normally use.

From Theory to Practice

▲ Usually there will be an alternative – albeit longer
– route to the hole for the less adventurous golfer
on a tough par three, but if there isn't, focus on
what you want to achieve, not what you don't want.

Long par three
(5th hole, 205yds)

There can't be anything that the average golfer finds more challenging than a death or glory short hole where he either carries the water or he doesn't. The first thing to observe here, is playing it off its full length is daft unless you're a very good player.

For a decent pro this would be a two or three iron off the back tees, so on this sort of hole you should be playing off the tees that would require you to use a four wood or three iron. The Oxfordshire, where these photographs were taken, has clearly thought of this: there are no less than seven tees to choose from!

There's no really smart strategy you can use on a hole like this. You've got to approach it with a positive frame of mind and dismiss the water from your thoughts. Clearly it is a mightily tough challenge, but you're up to it. Aren't you? Finally, swing smoothly. The smoother your swing is, the greater your chances of making the putting surface.

Short par three
(2nd hole, 141yds)

Typically a short par three will feature a small green that is heavily bunkered. Think of the Postage Stamp at Royal Troon, so named because of the size of the green, or the fourth at Turnberry. Miss either green and you are looking at a five not a three. And why not? You have got a short iron in your hands, so if you miss the target you should be heavily punished.

This is a short par three with a difference. It has a large green, but there isn't a great deal of depth to it, so you have to be wary. Clearly the sensible shot here is to aim for the fat of the green. Most players would kick themselves if they dropped a shot on a hole like this.

Because the hole is flat, this is one instance where you need to pay extra attention to its length. If you think it looks much shorter you will underclub, with disastrous consequences.

▲ Short par threes often have a sting in the tail somewhere, so always keep a look out for the hidden dangers on the tee.

▲ A wonderful par four, where the more you aim towards the bunkers on the left, the shorter your approach shot.

▲ Playing a long par four as a par five instead takes the pressure off and often rewards you with an unexpected par.

▶▶ On a long par four you need to hit a good tee shot to stand a chance of reaching the green in regulation figures.

Long par four (9th hole, 405 yds)

This is a classic long par four. It is a dog-leg left and so the more to the left you drive your ball the less distance you will have to travel with your approach shot. But the corner of the dog-leg is protected by bunkers so you have to tread carefully here. Similarly, if you play too safe, you will not only be too far away to reach the green in two, but you will be blocked out by the rolling hills on the right of the picture.

The green has a narrow entrance but widens and has plenty of depth, and is therefore very forgiving, so a player can be bold here. The advantages of taking as much off the dog-leg as you dare are such that you need to be aggressive off the tee. If you have the ability to fade the ball, this type of hole is perfect for you. Be brave; don't be afraid to line up on the bunker and let the ball fade back into the safety of the fairway.

Whenever you approach this type of green, you should consider using one club more than normal, as all the trouble is at the front of the green. The very narrow entrance means that, if you can, you should take it out of play.

Of course, 405yds may be outside your range in two anyway. Even if you can get up with your two Sunday-best shots, you should really play it as a par five. This is such a difficult par four that it is easy to score six in trying to obtain par. But it offers a straightforward chance to score five.

If you fit this bill you shouldn't be flirting with the bunkers on the left at all. Your approach should leave you about 70yds from the green and a simple pitch and two putts at the worst.

◄◄ Although short par fours often provide a good chance to make a birdie, they are often dangerous, too.

►► Playing to an elevated green, you will need to take at least one extra club to allow for the fact that the full flight of the ball is shortened.

Short par four (6th hole, 320yds)

Some of the best holes on any course are short par fours. Think of the 10th hole at the Belfry or the 12th at Sunningdale.

In recent years there has been a trend to do away with the short par four because some macho golf course designers think that, despite evidence to the contrary, that there is no place for them because the better players simply overpower them.

Thankfully the architect Rees Jones isn't a paid-up subscriber to this errant nonsense and he has come up with two beauties at the Oxfordshire. One is the 8th, where the player has to box clever around a lake, but the 6th is the sort of hole you might see on any good golf course, and so perhaps will serve our purposes better here.

The green is devilishly protected – they usually are on holes this length – and so the strategy here has to be to find the fairway with your tee shot. Ideally you want to leave yourself with a full nine iron or wedge shot, because that way you'll have more chance of stopping the ball.

The green is slightly elevated and so if you hit a nine iron 120yds and you have 120yds to play, you are really going to have to strike it well to get the distance. Short of the green is no place to be, so the smart play here should be a smooth eight iron, with your hands perhaps slightly further down the shaft than normal.

▲ Although a long par five may seem intimidating, the length of the hole usually means there are several ways of playing it successfully. Playing option 1 will enable you to avoid the bunkers on the right edge of the fairway even though it makes the hole a little longer.

Long par five (4th hole, 545yds)

This is a hole the like of which you may never have seen before! The middle of the fairway is dominated by a bunker that must be 80yds in length from back to front, so clearly some added thought is needed. The members at the Oxfordshire must be decent fairway bunker players.

The hole is a dog-leg right and therefore the object of the exercise is to drive the ball long enough to leave you the opportunity of clearing 'the desert' with your second shot.

One thing you mustn't do is be too greedy. A drive that finishes in the rough on the right, leaves a player looking at a six at best. Don't get intimidated by this type of hole. That's the effect the architect is trying to achieve. Be confident, and don't let the doubts creep into your mind. In fact if your drive finishes straight

down the middle, clearing the sand ought not to prove such a problem with your second shot.

What if your ball goes to the left and now you know you can't clear the sand with your second? You have to be honest with yourself: how good am I out of fairway bunkers? If they hold no terrors, then blast away and take your chances. A fairway bunker will only cost you 20yds at most and if you lay up short you're throwing away more than 80yds and you have no chance of reaching the green in three. If you're absolutely terrible, however (which you shouldn't be after reading this), you may consider it a price worth paying.

The green is narrow to the left with plenty to aim at on the right. The pin is invariably on the left. If you've a wedge in your hands and you're confident with it, you may think it worth having a go at the pin, otherwise, make sure you hit the green. A par five on a long, long hole is never a bad score.

Short par five (17th hole, 490yds)

Again, short par fives are invariably a focus for much excitement because of the possibility of scoring birdies and eagles. Augusta National has two classics with the 13th and the 15th, and the tournament is invariably won or lost on these two holes.

The 17th at the Oxfordshire is a perfect example of this type of hole. The penalties for someone who gambles and fails are severe, but the rewards for success are great.

In effect, there are two fairways, divided by an enormous water hazard. The boldest of drives allows you to cross the water for a relatively easy route for the rest of the hole. Indeed anyone who hits the ball a good length will be able to consider hitting the green in two shots. The other, safer option on the tee means the water is a factor for you for the rest of the hole.

Most players will have to go by this route. The glory offered by the first option is overwhelmed by the risk. Sure you could get a four. But you could easily be playing three from in front of the lake.

The trick on a hole like this is to try to dismiss the intimidating effects of the water from the mind. You've got plenty of room with your drive and also with your second shot, which leaves a straightforward pitch to the green. Why worry about the water?

The smartest ploy is to play the wood off the tee with which you feel most confident, to enable you to forget the lake on the left and hit the fairway. Now take a fairway wood or a long to medium iron – again the one with which you feel entirely comfortable – and pick out a spot where you want the ball to land and focus on it. The point about water holes is that once you've played them properly a couple of times, the fear element is then dramatically diminished. Thinking clearly is a big step in this direction.

▲ On a reachable par five, a calculated gamble off the tee may allow you to reach the green in two shots. The two best choices here are to go across the lake (1) or around it (2) – going around the lake is by far the safest option.

Glossary

ALBATROSS A score of three under par on a hole. In America it is referred to as a double-eagle.

BACK-NINE The second set of nine holes on an 18-hole golf course. Sometimes referred to as the inward nine.

BIRDIE A score of one under par on a hole.

BOGEY A score of one over par on a hole.

BORROW The amount a putt will deviate due to slope of the green.

BUNKER/SANDTRAP A sand-filled hole, usually placed on the edges of the fairway and around the greens.

CARRY The distance from when a ball is struck to when it first lands.

CHIP A low-running shot played from around the green to the putting surface.

DIVOT A piece of turf removed when a shot is played.

DOG-LEG A hole that changes direction, either to the left or the right, halfway through its course.

DRAW A specialist shot where the ball curves from right to left in the air. The opposit of a fade.

DRIVER The longest and least loted club in the bag. Normally used for teeing off on par fours or par fives. Also referred to as the 1-wood.

EAGLE A score of two under par on a hole.

FADE A specialist shot where the ball curves from left to right in the air. The opposite of a draw.

FAIRWAY The area of mown turf between tee and green.

FOURBALL A match between two teams of two players, each playing their own ball.

FOURSOME A match between two teams of two players, each playing one ball by alternate shots.

FRINGE The area of of fairly short grass between the green and the fairway.

FRONT NINE The opening nine holes on an 18-hole golf course. Sometimes referred to as the outward nine.

GREEN An area of closely-mown grass prepared for putting.

HANDICAP The system than enables players both to take on each other and the course on level terms. The worse a player is, the higher the handicap and the more shots he receives. If someone regularly goes around a course in 20 over par then they should have a handicap of 20 and will receive 20 shots towards their efforts of matching the par of the course.

HICKORY An old type of wood once used to manufacture golf shafts.

HOOK A mistimed shot that deviates severely to the left for the right-handed player.

LIE Situation in which a ball finishes after the playing of a stroke.

LONG IRON A description for those irons numbered one to four.

MATCHPLAY Form of the game where holes won and lost are the determining factor rather than strokes played.

MID-IRON A description for those irons numbered five to seven.

OUT OF BOUNDS Normally highlighted by a series of white stakes, the area of the course which is outside the boundry lines. Golfers incur a penalty stroke and have to replay their shot again if their ball flies out of bounds.

PAR The standard score for each hole, and the entire course.

PITCH Lofted shot from around the green to the putting surface.

PITCHMARK The indentation caused when the ball lands on the green after an approach shot.

R & A The game's governing body, the Royal and Ancient Golf Club of St Andrews.

ROUGH The area of unmown grass that lies either side of the fairway.

SHORT IRON A description for those irons numbered eight to nine, the pitching wedge, sand wedge, and indeed any other wedges.

SHANK Totally mistimed shot, usually with a short iron, where the ball comes off the junction between hosel and club-face and travels at right angles to the target intended.

SLICE Mistimed shot where the ball deviates sharply to the right for the right-handed player.

STROKEPLAY Form of the game where the number of strokes played is the determining factor.

SWEET SPOT The precise spot in the middle of the club where the greatest possible mass can be delivered from the club face to the ball.

TEE Closely-mown area where the first stroke on a hole is played. The ball is generally played from a tee peg.

YIPS A nervous condition induced by poor chipping and putting which can render its victim totally unable to do either.

Index

Acknowledgements

Allsport 148, 149 right/Brian Bahr 80, 115/David Cannon 20, 21, 22, 144, 176/Jon Ferrey 127/Harry How 17 bottom, 28/Craig Jones 154 top/Ross Kinnaird 109/Andy Lyons 24 right/Donald Miralle 15, 16/Stephen Munday 39, 174, 175/Andrew Redington 29, 40 left, 62, 151 bottom/Dave Rogers 81/Paul Severn 61, 63 bottom, 139, 154 bottom, 179

Bridgeman Art Library, London/New York/British Museum, London 10/National Gallery, London 8

Golf Picture Bank /Nick Walker 19, 44 left, 44 right, 45, 145, 178

Ben Hogan UK 79

Octopus Publishing Group Limited 27 top, 27 bottom, 34 bottom, 36-37, 38, 114, 128, 168/Mark Newcombe 32, 40 right, 41 left, 41 right, 58, 96 bottom, 100 left, 100 right, 100 centre, 101, 122 left, 122 right, 122 centre, 123/Nick Walker front cover right, back cover, 1, 2, 3, 7, 42 left, 42 right, 43 left, 43 right, 43 centre, 46 left, 46 right, 46 centre, 47, 48 left, 48 right, 49 left, 49 right, 50, 52 left, 52 right, 52 centre, 53 left, 53 right, 59, 64-65, 68 left, 68 right, 68 centre, 69 left, 69 right, 70 left, 70 right, 72 left, 72 right, 73, 74 left, 76 left, 76 right, 76 centre, 77, 82 left, 82 right, 82 centre, 84 left, 84 right, 85, 86 left, 86 right, 87 left, 87 right, 88 left, 88 right, 88 centre, 89, 90 left, 90 right, 90 centre, 90-91, 92 left, 92 right, 92 centre, 94 left, 94 right, 95, 96 top, 97 left, 97 right, 98 left, 98 right, 99 left, 99 right, 102, 103, 104 left, 104 right, 105, 106, 107 left, 107 right, 107 centre, 108, 112 left, 112 right, 119, 120 left, 120 right, 121 right, 121 centre, 124, 125, 126, 129, 130, 131 left, 131 right, 132, 133 left, 133 right, 134, 136 left, 136 right, 140, 146 top, 146 bottom, 156, 158 left, 158 right, 158 centre, 158-159, 162 left, 162 centre, 163, 164 left, 164 right,164 centre, 165, 166 left, 166 right, 166 centre, 167 left, 167 right, 167 centre, 170 left, 170 right, 170 centre, 171 top, 171 bottom right, 171 bottom left, 171 bottom centre, 180, 181, 182 top left, 182 top right, 182 bottom, 183 top, 183 bottom, 184, 184 inset, 162 right

Science Photo Library/NASA 177

Phil Sheldon front cover left, 9, 11, 12, 13, 17 top, 23 top, 23 bottom, 24 left, 30 top, 30 bottom, 31, 33 top, 33 bottom, 34 top, 35, 37, 54, 57, 60, 63 top, 67, 71, 74 right, 78, 111, 113, 116, 117, 118, 135, 138, 142, 143, 149 left, 151 top, 155, 157, 160, 160-161, 169, 172, 173/M. Harris 14/Jan Traylen 18, 141

Taylor Made 26 left, 26 right, 36, 54-55, 55, 56

Roger Tidman 152, 153

Executive editor	Julian Brown
Editor	Abi Rowsell
Senior designer	Joanna Bennett
Designer	Bill Mason
Picture researchers	Charlotte Dean and Maria Gibbs
Production Controller	Viv Cracknell
Indexer	Hilary Bird